FOLK TALES OF THE SANTALS

FOLK TALES OF THE SANTALS

INDU ROY CHAUDHURY

GYAN

ISBN: 978-81-212-1392-9(HB)

First Published in 1960
Indian Reprint in 2017

Published by

Gyan Publishing House
5, Ansari Road
Daryaganj, New Delhi-110002
Phone: 9811692060
E-mail: books@gyanbooks.com

Cataloging in Publication Data—DK
Courtesy: D.K. Agencies (P) Ltd. <docinfo@dkagencies.com>

Roy Chaudhury, Indu, 1903- **author.**
Folk tales of the Santals / Indu Roy Chaudhury.
pages cm
Reprint. Originally published: New Delhi : Sterling Publishers Pvt Ltd, 1973.
ISBN 9788121213929 (HB)

1. Santal (South Asian people)—Folklore. 2. Tales—India. I. Title.

PZ8.1.R842Fo 2017 DDC 398.20899595 23

GENERAL EDITOR'S INTRODUCTION

Folklore in the different parts of India is a rich legacy for us. While researches in ancient and modern history have been directed in recent decades more to the succession of kings and political shifts, not much notice has been paid to the culture, complex traditions and social beliefs of the common people. The sociologists have also to pay a good deal of attention to the customs and beliefs of the people and changes therein through the ages. They have rather neglected the study of folklore which is a reliable index to the background of the people. There has always been an easy mobility of folklore through pilgrimages, *melas* and fairs. The wandering minstrels, *sadhus* and *fakirs* have also disseminated them. People of the North visiting the temples of the South and *vice versa* carry their folk tales, songs, riddles and proverbs with them and there is an inconspicuous integration. The *dharamsdas*, inns and the *chattis* (places of rest where the pilgrims rest and intermingle) worked as the clearing house for the folk tales, traditional songs and riddles. That is why we find a somewhat common pattern in folk literature of different regions. The same type of folk tale will be found in Kashmir and in Kerala with slight regional variation. These stories were passed on from generation to generation by word of mouth before they came to be reduced to writing.

Folklorists have different approaches to the appreciation of folklore. Max Mueller has interpreted the common pattern in folk literature as evidence of nature-myths. Sir L. Gomme thought that a historical approach is the best for the study of folklore. But Frazer would rather encourage a commonsense approach and to him, old and popular folk literature is mutually interdependent and satisfies the basic curiosities and instincts of man. That folklore is a vital element in a living culture has been underlined in recent years by scholars like Malinowski and Radcliffe Brown.

It is unfortunate that the study of folklore in India is of very recent origin. This is all the more regrettable because the *Panchatantra* stories which had their origin in Bihar had spread through various channels almost throughout the world. As late as in 1859, T. Benfey had held that there is an unmistakable stamp of Indian origin in most of the fairy tales of Europe. The same stories with different twists or complexes have come back to us through Grimm and Aesop and the retold stories are greedily swallowed by our children. That India has neglected a proper study of the beautiful motifs of our folk tales is seen in the fact that the two large volumes of the dictionary of Folklore, Mythology and Legend published by Messrs Funk and Wagnalls and Company of New York have given a very inadequate reference to India.

What is the secret of the fascination of the folk tales that the old, the young and children are kept enthralled by their recitals? The same story is often repeated but does not lose its interest. The secret is the satisfaction that our basic curiosity finds in the folk tales. The folk tales through phantasies, make-belief and complacent understanding help primitive man to satisfy his curiosity about the mysteries of the world and particularly the very many inexplicable phenomena of nature around him. We have an element of primitiveness in our mind in spite of the advancement of science around us. Even a scientist finds great delight in the fairy tales of the moon being attacked as the origin of the lunar eclipse. Through the folk tales man exercised his once-limited vision and somehow or the other we would like to retain that limited vision even when we have grown up. The advancement in science can never replace the folk tales. On the other hand, folk tales have helped the scientific curiosity of men. In spite of the scientific explanation as to why earthquakes take place, the old, the young and children would still be delighted to be told that the world rests on the hood of a great snake and when the snake is tired with its weight, it shakes the hood and there is an earthquake. Among the Mundas, an aboriginal tribe in Bihar, there is a wonderful explanation of the constellation Orion. The sword and belt of Orion, the Mundas imagined, form their appropriate likeness to the plough and plough-share which the supreme *Sing Bonga* God first shaped in the heavens and then taught people on earth how to use the plough and the plough-share. It is further said in the Munda folk tale that while the *Sing Bonga* was shaping the plough and the plough-share with a chisel and a hammer he observed a dove hatching its eggs at a little distance. The *Sing Bonga* threw his hammer at the dove to bag the game. He missed his mark and the hammer went over the dove's head and hung on a tree. The hammer corresponds to the Pleiads which resembles a hammer. The Aldebaran is the dove and the other stars of Hyades are the eggs of the dove. Any illiterate Munda boy will unmistakably point out these star groups.

Weather and climate have their own stories and are often connected with particular stage of the crops. The wet season and the hottest month are intimately associated with the ripening of crops or the blossoming of trees or the frequency of dust storms and stories are woven round them. But nothing is more satisfying as a folk story than the explanation of the phases of the stars, moon and the sun. A Munda would point out the milky way as the *Gai Hora* i.e. path of the cows. The *Sing Bonga* God leads his cows every day along this path—the dusky path on the sky is due to the dust raised by the herd. The dust raised by the cows sends down the rains. A story of this type can never fail to sustain its interest in spite of all the scientific explanation of the astral bodies.

The "why and wherefore" of the primitive mind tried to seek an answer in the surrounding animal and plant kingdom. Animals are grouped into different categories according to their intelligence and other habits. The fox is always sly while the cow is gentle. The lion and the tiger have a majestic air while the horse is swift, sleek and intelligent. The slow-going elephant does not forget its attendant nor does he forget a man that teases him. Monkeys are very close to man. The peacock is gay while the crow is shrewd. The tortoise is slow-going but surefooted. The hare is swift but apt to laze on the road. The primitive mind has enough intelligence to decipher these inherent characteristics of the common animals he meets. Similarly, when he sees a large and shady peepal tree he naturally regards it as the abode of the sylvan god. The thick jungle with its trees and foliage is known to be frequented by thieves and dacoits. Any solitary hut in the heart of the forest must be associated with someone unscrupulous or uncanny. These ideas are commonly woven into stories and through them the primitive mind seeks to satisfy the eternal why and how of the mind. Folk literature is often crude and even grotesque. The stories of the witches and the ogres come in this category. There is nothing to be surprised at that. They reflect the particular stage of the development of the human mind and also are a projection of the beliefs and fads of the mind.

Scientific accuracy should never be looked for in folk tales although folk tales are a very good reflex of the social developments of a particular time.

It is enough if the basic ideas regarding the animal and plant kingdom still satisfy that the donkey is dense or stupid and the snake typifies slyness and the fox is deceitful. These ideas repeated in ancient folk tales have stood the test of time and this would show that the primitive mind was not foolish or credulous. The very idea that the folk tales have woven man, nature, animal and plant creation together shows the great flight of imagination and a singular development of mind. Introduction of moral lessons or any dogma was not done as an after-thought but came in as a very natural development.

The last source of the folk tales is human society itself. The clemental moorings that are at the root of human society are sought to be illustrated in folk tales. The day-to-day life of the common man finds its full depiction in the folk tales. Parental love, family happiness, children's adventurous habits, love and fear of the unknown, greed etc. are some of the usual themes of folk tales. The common man yearns for riches and comforts he cannot usually look for. He dreams of riches, princes, kingdoms etc. and finds satisfaction in stories of fantasy. Men love gossip and scandal. Women cannot keep secrets, children will love their parents, a mother-in-law will always think the daughter-in-law needs to be told what to do—these are some of the basic ideas that make up much of our daily life. The folk tales are woven round them and whether fantastic or with a moral undertone they only reflect the daily chores, tears and joys of the common man.

Unknowingly, the folklorists bring in the religious customs, beliefs, food habits, modes of dress, superstitions etc. and thereby leave a picture of the culture-complex of the region and its people. A tribal story does not picture a king riding a white big foaming horse followed by hundreds of other horsemen going for a *shikar*. In a tribal story the Raja will be found cutting the grass and bringing back a stack of it to feed his cows, but a folk tale more current in urban areas will have large palaces, liveried servants, ministers and courtiers in the king's court. All this only means that the time and the venue of the origin of the stories are widely different. It is here that the sociologists and the anthropologists come in useful. As life is different in rural and urban areas or is chequered with goodness or badness in the world so is folk literature diversified, as it must be, being a replica of life.

It is a pity that these beautiful folk tales in India were almost on the point of disappearance when a few pioneers mostly consisting of foreign missionaries and European scholars looked into them and made compilations in different parts of India. Our present run of grandmothers know very little of them. The professional story tellers who were very dearly sought after by the old and the young, not to speak of the children, have almost completely disappeared from India. The film industry and the film songs pose a definite threat to folklore.

The Sterling Publishers are to be congratulated for launching the project of publishing a compilation of 20 volumes consisting of the folk tales of different regions. The work has been entrusted to specially selected writers who have an intimate knowledge of their region. The regional complex of the stories has been sought to be preserved as far as possible. The stories have an elemental involvement about them and they are such as are expected to appeal to the child and its parents. We expect the reader of the folk tales of the particular region to feel, after reading the stories, that he has enjoyed a whiff of the air of that area. We want him to have an idea of how Kashmiri folks retire in wintry night with the *Kangri* under the folds of their clothes to enjoy a gossip and how they enjoy their highly spiced meaty food. We want him to appreciate the splash of the colours of the sari and the flowers that are a must in Tamil Nadu. We want him to know the stories that are behind some of the famous temples in the South such as the Kanjeevaram temple. We want him to know the story regarding the construction of the famous Konark temple. We want him to enjoy the stories of the heroes of Gujarat, Punjab and Rajasthan in their particular roles. We want the reader to have an idea of the peace and quiet of a hut in the lap of the Kumaon hills. We want the reader to enjoy some of the folk tales of Bengal and Bihar that have found wings in other parts of India and to appreciate the village life with its *Alpana* and *Bratas*. At the same time we want the reader to appreciate the customs and manners of the Santals, Garos, and the other tribes inhabiting NEFA and Assam.

A set of twenty volumes of folk tales of the different regions of India by selected authors is an ambitious programme. Folk tales have great impact in bringing in national integration of the country. A Keralite will see a pattern of familiarity while reading the folk tales of Bengal, Assam and Kashmir. Maharashtra and Orissa will come nearer to each other through ties of folk tales. The reader will feel that he is at one with his brother or sister elsewhere. A spread of knowledge of the social patterns of the different regions is a pre-requisite for national integration. It can be modestly claimed that this folk tales series will be of great help in that direction. The publishers want to have a miniature India in these 20 volumes.

The tribals of India form an important element in India's teeming population. With a certain affinity in the culture of the tribals, their folk tales have a basic familiarity, whether in Arunachal (previously NEFA), Nagaland, Orissa, Bihar or Madhya Pradesh. A book on Santal folk tales will give the reader a good idea of the tribals' fears, dreams and desires and their culture-complex. That is why the inclusion of Santal folk tales in this series. The Santals are the only tribe that is found in different parts of India.

The author has given a good description of the Santals in her preface. I may add that in 1855 the Santals had spearheaded an insurrection against the *Dikkus* (foreigners), the money-lenders and the unsympathetic bureaucracy. With bows and arrows they had faced the bullets of the administration. They were, in a way, pioneers in the struggle for India's freedom.

The tribals in India are now at a crossroad. Their culture-complex is shedding many of the basic features. It is high time their folklore is preserved. In this context, and for the integration of the different parts of India with very many ethnic groups, this book on Santal folk tales has a special role to perform. I am sure the author has enjoyed the assignment. She has helped to make out a miniature India in the twenty volumes of this series. It is hoped the reader will enjoy the stories and come to know more of their manners and customs, the various forms of marriage, their implicit faith in spirits etc. Most villages mentioned in the stories are situated in the district of Santal Parganas, a picturesque region in India. I have heard some of the stories in the tea gardens of Assam from the lips of the Santal tea-labourers and also from the Santal labourers who have settled down in the foothills of the Himalayas on the Nepal frontier. The record and readership of these fine stories will surely lead to national integration.

P. C. Roy Chaudhury

PREFACE

The Santals, a virile and colourful tribe of Santal Parganas district in Bihar have spread into several other districts in Bihar as well as the neighbouring States. They are found in Assam and Kerala. The Santals are devoted to music and dance and they love the open—the open hills and the forests. Excellent in reclaiming lands, they are extremely hardy but are a very carefree tribe. A cheerful lot, if they have just enough to eat and drink, they will spend more on religious and social ceremonies. They love to explore the hills and the jungles with their axe, bows and arrows. They would eat almost all kinds of animals, both domestic and non-domestic –birds, fish and jungle tubers, leaves and fruits. They love relaxing and would dance through the night with music from the flute, *Mudal* (big drum) and other musical instruments. The women are extremely gay. Their social system is regulated by tribal laws and they are under strict discipline of the Panchayats and the social and the religious Heads.

They are neat and clean. It is a pleasure to see their huts with plastered and painted mud-walls. The position of women is well-defined and they have their particular civil rights and some of them extend to a quick divorce in case of non-compatibility of temperament. They believe in witch-craft and the *Bongas* (spirits), taboos and sympathetic magic. They have the idea of a Supreme-being and they live in complete harmony with the surroundings with no temple and idol for worship. The Santals' surroundings—the hill, the dale, the spring, the sacred groves—are the objects of their reverential fear. They have a harmonious life under the belief in the supernatural influence of the *Bongas* and witches. They believe in a number of good and bad spirits with the supreme deity whether known as the *Thakur Jiu* or the *Marang Buru* at the Head. There are twelve clans among the Santals with distinct totems. Their religious ceremonies and festivals form most part of their life.

The Santal folk tales reflect their faithfulness and under

line their chief characteristics in religious and social spheres. They love to hear folk tales, riddles and bits of folk songs. Their folk tales have cut across the boundaries of their country and it is not strange that some of the tales are in common with those that are found in other parts of India. Their kings are simple villagers and do not move about in chariots drawn by white-foaming horses. The kings go and cut grass or collect fuel. Living in the midst of jungles and mountains, many of their folk tales are based on animal stories. Their religious and social customs are reflected in some of their folk tales. One can distinguish the later folk tales from the earlier folk tales, as there has been a great change among the Santals as well. In the grazing fields or in the *akharas* (dancing floors) Santal boys sit or lie and one of them recites a story and then others repeat the process. Witchcraft stories or stories of the *Bongas,* animals changing into human form and *vice versa, Ojhas* (witch doctors) naturally excite them a lot. The Santal folk tales present their mythology as well. These folk tales have been a treasure with them which has been carried to the tea-plantations in Assam or the coffee-plantations in Kerala. Trend of industrialisation and modernisation has started creating a havoc with the even tenor of life of the Santals and many of the folk tales are getting lost. The villages mentioned in the stories retold here are still in existence and the villagers believe the tales to be true.

It is the Missionaries of the Scandinavian Mission to the Santals that have done a great service by collecting many of their stories and legends. The earlier pioneers in this line were Rev O.Bodding, and Rev Dr Campbell. Some of the earlier administrators of Santal Parganas like Mr C.H. Bompas, I.C.S. also felt a great interest in collecting the stories.

In order to understand the Santal folk stories, it is necessary to know a bit of the geography of the Santal Parganas. This is a very large district extending over 5,470 sq. miles and on the boundaries are districts of Bengal, and a few other districts of Bihar. The district is an upland tract with a hilly backbone cutting it from north to south. Certain hills rise abruptly from the plains. The district is a hilly portion, a portion of rolling nature with jungles and also a large part of flat country. The scenery is variegated with hills, dales, forests, rivers, water springs and also un-reclaimed *tanr* lands (uplands). The district has some minerals and interesting fauna and flora. The predominant tree in the district which has a religious sanctity for the Santals is the *Sal (Shorea robusta)*. Their *Sarna* is a sacred *Sal* grove where their gods live. *Sabai* grass which is used for making paper is grown on hills of the Rajmahal Range. The fauna comprises tigers, leopards, bears, deer and wild-pig. There are hundreds of types of game-birds and reptiles. Fish forms an attractive dish for the Santals.

The Santal folk tales have an entity of their own and only a few of them have been retold in this book.

Indu Roy Chaudhury

CONTENTS

1

THE ORIGIN OF THE WORLD

WHEN there were no men and women, no animals and birds, no trees and mountains, this great world of ours contained only water and water everywhere. At some places floating like a blue sheet of water while elsewhere roaring mighty foamy waves. But there was no life to witness the varied moods of nature.

Thakur Jiu or *Thakur Baba* (the greatest of the gods) thought: "This is a great world, but there must be living creatures." So God created a few water animals, like the crocodile and the crab tortoise. Then God thought of creating men and women. He brought out some muddy earth from the bottom of the water and made two human forms. But just when *Thakur Jiu* was going to breathe life into the human form, a big fiery horse came down from the scorching sun and kicked the two earthen images that broke into pieces. The horse was sent by the Sun-god who did not want any man or woman in the world.

Thakur Jiu thought again: "Before I create man and woman, let me create some birds that would flap the wings, some solid land, trees and bushes. Or else how and where will the birds make their nests ?"

So *Thakur Jiu* ordered the crocodile, lobster and the whale to bring up earth and create a surface. But as soon as they deposited the particles of earth on the surface the water washed them away.

This was a problem.

Thakur Jiu asked the earth-worm to bring earth and put it on the back of the tortoise and asked the tortoise to float on the surface of water. This the tortoise did and the earth-worm started eating the soil with its mouth and pushed it out from the hind portion and the earth was put on the back of the tortoise. In this way countless of tortoises and earth-worms worked day and night and created a surface of soil. Then *Thakur Jiu* created a couple of big birds and put a number of trees, tall and strong and a large number of bushes.

This is how the world and the earth came into existence. Then *Thakur Jiu* asked the birds to make their nests. The birds followed the instructions. Two large, shining, white eggs were laid. When the eggs were hatched a smiling boy and a lovely girl came out. The birds got frightened and flapped their wings and came to *Thakur Jiu*. "Oh *Thakur Jiu*, come and see—the eggs have not produced birds". Then *Thakur Jiu* smiled and said : "Yes, I know, they are a boy and a girl but they will be growing into a man and a woman."

They grew up and came to be known as Pilchu-Haram and Pilchu-Burhi. They did not have any clothes on. *Thakur Jiu* then made a strong drink which they drank. They came to get their sense of shame, made clothes out of bark and lived as man and wife.

They had a number of children and each one of them created a family. They were known as the Santals. The land surface created by the tortoises and earth-worms was too small for them. The Santals started migrating as by that time the land surface had also become larger. This is how the world was created and the Santals came into being.

The children multiplied and the surplus population started moving from place to place. For some time they lived close to Harata but moved from there to a flat riverside land (*Beda*) with turmeric (*sasan*). This area was known as Sasan-Beda. Here the Santals were divided into tribes and on their onward march they came across a very high range of hills. In trying to cross the hills they nearly lost their lives. The hills were so high that it was long into the forenoon that the Santals could see the sun—a proof that they were travelling east in order to be saved from the difficulties of crossing the high ranges of hills. They started worshipping *Marang Buru* (the big mountain). On and on hey moved and finally came to Chai country from where they moved to Champa.

Champa was under the Santals for a long time and they lived in peace with the Hindus as the Santals had helped Rama against Ravana. But later fight began with the Hindus and among the Santals themselves. More and more tribes were created out of the Santals—Mundas, Birhors etc. They again had to move out and the Santals at length found themselves on the table-land of Chhota Nagpur in Bihar and the over-flow population came to the area now known as the Santal Parganas. From here they spread to areas like Birbhum in Bengal, Singhbhum and Palamau districts in Bihar.

The Santals also worshipped *Thakur* (God). In ancient times, the rice grew ready-husked and the cotton bushes bore cloth all ready woven. The Santals were clean and they did not have to pick the lice out of each other's hair. But a Santal serving-girl of one of the Raja of Champa was very dirty in her habits. When she would be cleaning out a cow-house, she would wipe them on the cloth she was wearing. Without cleaning herself properly in the morning she would pick and eat the rice. *Thakur Baba* got angry and ordered that the rice should grow in a husk and the cotton plants would produce raw-cotton and men would have to card and weave.

In those good old days, the sky was quite close to the earth and occasionally *Thakur Baba* would come and visit men in their houses. He asked them not to throw dirty leaf-plates near the front or back-door and not to let the brass-plates and dishes remain unwashed at night. But one day *Thakur Baba* came and found used leaf-plates collected at the doors of the Santals. *Thakur Baba* got very angry and stopped visiting his children very often. But the men will not take the lesson and continued in their dirty habits. *Thakur Baba* resolved to destroy them all.

Thakur Baba is *Sing Chando* or the Sun and Moon is his wife. Stars are their children. Sing Chando blazed with fierce heat till all men and beasts writhed and prayed and prayed. *Thakur Baba* was approached by the Moon not to destroy the men. But Sing Chando said he had already taken a vow to destroy all men but he would spare the race. He chose out a young man and a young woman and bade them to go into a cave in a hill-side. The passage of the cave was closed with raw-hide. Only these two were saved and the fire that rained for five days and five nights killed all others.

However, these two raised a new race. The Moon was very kind to them and used to hide the new born babies in a large basket and smeared the mouth of the basket with mud. In this way the Santals were preserved and they are today a hardy race with simple habits and joyous nature.

2

HOW TIME WAS DIVIDED INTO DAY AND NIGHT

AT the beginning of the world, there was no moon. The sun was alone in the sky and did never set.

One day the Supreme God came down to the world and found that a man was making fields. The man did not realize that he was facing the Supreme God as the God had taken the shape of a fellow man. The God asked : "When did you make this field ?" The man answered : "I made it now."

The God asked again : "When did you make the adjoining field ?"

The man replied : "I made it now."

The God pointed out some fields at a little distance and said : "When did you make yonder fields ?"

The man again said : "I made all those fields just now, Sir "

The God was puzzled. He saw that there were some leaf-plates from which the man had eaten. The God asked him : "When did you eat from these fresh leaf-plates ?"

The man answered : "Now."

The God pointed to a few dry leaf-plates at a distance from which the man had eaten some time back. So he asked the man again as to when had he eaten in those dried leaves. The reply was again the same : "Now."

The God was still more puzzled. Then the God asked : "My dear man, when do you work and when do you rest ?"

The man answered : "I rest now and I work now. There is no other time than *now*. When else could I rest ?"

The God's eyes opened. He understood that He must make some arrangement by which his men would get some definite time for work and definite time for rest The God told the man : "Well, in future you will have plenty of time to rest. I shall make the night for you to rest."

The man replied : "Sir, I do not understand what the night is, and who are you that you say that you will make the night ?" The God smiled and vanished.

The God sent for the sun and said : "You must not always shine. Because if you do that there is no division of time and man works and eats at any time and does not know when to rest. If this goes on the man will die of sheer work. So you have to hide yourself for as long as you shine. When you hide, man will not be able to see anything and so he will rest."

From then onwards the sun started setting in the evening. This made the earth dark. Man was wonder-struck. He could see nothing and had no option but to finish his work for the day. But this darkness also amounted to the man's falling into ditches and hunting himself. Man now began to work with the sun rise and stopped with the sun set.

The God came to the man again and said : "Now you know what night is. When there is light, work; when it is night, rest, and on the morrow you work again, and rest again when night comes". By that time the man had understood that it was the *Sing Bonga* (Supreme Deity) that had come. The man made his *johar* (salutations) and said : "Master, I understand. But you speak of the morrow—what does it mean ?" The God replied : "I call today the time of light before the night comes, and I call the morrow, the time that will follow the night." The man did his *johar* again and said : "Master, I have understood. I will work and rest according to your command but there is one small difficulty."

The God wanted to know the difficulty. The man said : "Sir, when the night came I stopped working but on my way home I fell more than once into a ditch. It was all dark. How am I expected to reach home safely and have my meals ?"

The God realized the limitations of the change he had brought about. He thought that an alternative arrangement will have to be made. He said : "Alright, I shall arrange and the moon will come up to give you all a little light during the night; by the moon's light, you will be able to go about in the night." The God disappeared.

This then brought in force the appearance of moon in the night to give some light to the world.

3

HOW SABAI GRASS CAME IN

THE Sabai is a type of grass that grows wild on tops of hills in the Santal Parganas. The inhabitants of the hill-tops are known as 'Paharias' who are also a different kind of the tribals in that area. The Paharias are experts in growing Sabai grass and they cut down the grass when it is tall. The Sabai grass is used extensively for making paper. The Paharias do not want to go to the plains and would bring down on their heads the Sabai grass on the weekly market days and sell the grass at the village '*hats*' (markets). This story is very common as to the origin of the Sabai grass.

Long long ago there lived a family of six brothers and a sister. The brothers would spend their days in the jungle, hunting rabbits and deer or wild fowls while the sister would remain in the house and do the domestic chores. The sister was good in cooking and the brothers liked her cooking very much. One day while the brothers were going out there was nothing in the house to cook and the brothers wanted her to cook rice and wild *Sag* (Spinach). When the brothers were away the sister went round the village pond and collected some *Sag* that usually grows in the water of the ponds. While she was cutting the *Sag* into small pieces for cooking she cut her finger and a few drops of blood fell on the *Sag*. When the brothers returned the cooked *Sag* was served and the brothers found the *Sag* extremely tasty. They remarked about the extra taste in the *Sag* and wanted to know if she had used any special *Masala* (condiments). The sister said there was nothing unusual but a few drops of blood from her finger had fallen into the *Sag*.

When the brothers were left to themselves some of them suggested that if only a few drops of blood could make the *Sag* so tasty her flesh would be more delicious. The brothers thought they should kill her and eat her up. Lita, the youngest brother was not a party to the decision but he could not oppose the elders and kept quiet. Next morning the brothers took their sister with them and asked her to climb a tree and pluck the beautiful flowers of seven colours that had grown on the creeper on the tree. The girl did not suspect anything and climbed the tree. The six brothers shot her with arrows and Lita feigned that he was also shooting arrows but he saw to it that the arrows missed her. The sister was, however, killed.

The brothers sliced the body and asked Lita to get some fresh water. Lita sat down by the well and wept. When he was weeping a large frog came out of the water and asked him : "Lita why do you weep ? Can I help you ?" Lita told him as to what had happened. The frog said : "Please do not worry. I will give you a large *Rahu* fish and you cook it and hide the pieces of your sister's body. When the brothers go out for hunting you stay back on some excuse and bring the pieces of the body to the well and join them up. I will revive your sister."

The frog made over a large Rahu fish to Lita. Lita did exactly as the frog had told him. He cooked the Rahu fish and served it and the brothers liked the Rahu fish very much and said they had done well in killing the sister who tasted so nice. After a hearty meal they all went out for hunting but Lita stayed back stating that he would clean the house and also tend the *buffalo* which had a sore on its foot. The brothers left leaving Lita. Lita took the pieces of the sister's body to the well and the frog came out. The pieces were put in shape and the frog uttered some *Mantras* (incantations) and the sister sprang up alive. Lita left the house with sister and went to another jungle and started living there, as advised by the frog.

Sometime after a Raja came to the jungle where Lita and the sister lived and saw the girl. The girl had grown into a beautiful woman and the Raja at once fell in love with her. He took her away in order to marry her. He also took Lita with him and gave him half of his kingdom and his sister in marriage.

The brothers of Lita became poorer and poorer and had to earn a living by working as day labourers. The Raja decided to dig out an enormous tank so that the villagers could always have a supply of water, even if the rains failed. Hundreds of labourers from different villages came to dig the tank. Among them came Lita's five brothers. The sister recognized them and sent for them and the brothers were much afraid as to why the queen had sent for them. When they came and saw that the queen was no other than their sister they started weeping and asked for her pardon. The sister pardoned them and gave them gold, silver and clothes but the brothers were very repentant and would not take the presents. They squatted on the ground and started beating it with their hands as a mark of repentance and tears rolled down their eyes. As they were doing this suddenly the earth opened and swallowed them up but their long hair stuck out of the ground which joined up and the hair became Sabai grass. This is how Sabai grass originated which is now the mainstay of the Paharias on the hill tops of the Santal Pargana hills.

4

HOW A BRIDE WAS WON

BRIDE price has to be paid in the land of the Santals for winning a bride. There are various ways through which a bride is won. One such arrangement is that the prospective father-in-law gets a poor man as a plough boy or to help generally in the domestic chores for a stipulated period. During this period he is treated like a servant, although he is a member of the family and gets his food and clothing. He is not paid any wages. The bride price will be the wages in money value for the period the man works as a servant. But it is difficult to get a proper person who will be willing to work as a plough boy for a stipulated period and then marry the daughter of the house.

A Santal had five daughters but no son. He had a large area of cultivable land. At the time of cutting the crops or the threshing of the crops he was always in great difficulty as he did not have any son and he did not like to incur the expenses of engaging a day-labourer. He gave out that if a man would come and spend a night on the threshing floor with only one piece of cloth on him he would give one of his daughters in marriage. No one would accept the offer.

The story of the offer passed from village to village and a poor man was attracted. He did not have a second piece of cloth on him and had to engage himself as a labourer from village to village for his living. He took the offer and agreed to pass the night on the threshing floor with only one piece of cloth on him. It was mid-winter and the interior of the Santal Parganas gets very chilly in the night, particularly the straw on the threshing floor. The man was taken to be crazy to accept the offer in mid-winter. But having accepted the offer, there was no way out for the villager.

The labourer spent the night on the threshing floor with only one cloth on and braved the frost. Next morning he was accepted as a servant in the household of the villager and the stipulated period was only two years. He became the son-in-law of the family after the lapse of this period. At first the villager was very much annoyed that he had to give away his daughter to such a poor Santal but he found that the servant was very hard working and had pleasing manners. When the marriage was over, both the parties thought they had made a bargain.

5

THE BONGA'S VICTIM

ONCE upon a time there were seven brothers and one sister. The brothers were devoted to each other and to the sister but the wives did not like the sister. The wives used to poison the ears of their husbands at every possible opportunity that the sister was lazy and would not help in any domestic work. In this way, to some extent, the brothers were slowly alienated from the sister.

It was a regular habit of the brothers to go out hunting, leaving their wives and sister at home. On a particular hot day the brothers felt very thirsty as they had been hunting since dawn. They badly wanted some water to quench their thirst. One of the brothers climbed up a tree and from the top of the tree, he noticed a beautiful shining pool of water closeby. He came down and took the brothers to the direction where he had seen the water-pool. But they soon found that the water-pool was going further and further away from them as they were walking towards it. They realized that it was just a mirage and that some *Bonga* was deluding them. They thought they must offer some sacrifice to the *Bonga*.

The brothers discussed as to who should be sacrificed. No one offered to sacrifice his wife. They decided to sacrifice their only sister. Then the brothers offered a prayer to the *Bonga* that they will sacrifice their sister and the water-pool should be brought nearer to them. In moments they found the water-pool at a little distance from them and the brothers fully quenched their thirst.

The brothers went back home and a few days later they decided that the time had come for the sacrifice. The two youngest brothers begged for a little delay as they were still fond of their sister. The elder brothers agreed. Soon after one of the elder brothers fell seriously ill and no medicine could cure him. Then an *Ojha* (witch-doctor) was called and he found that the *Bonga* who had been promised something was causing all the illness and that if the vow was not fulfilled, the brother would surely die. The brothers secretly agreed that they will not make any further delay and asked the *Bonga* to give back the ailing brother. Suddenly the illness left the brother.

The brothers went to the same spot for hunting and asked their wives to send their sister with the breakfast. The pond was there. The sister came with the food and gave it to the brothers. They asked her to draw some water from the pond. The sister put her water-pot down to the surface but it would not sink so as to let the water fill into the earthen pot. The girl called out to her brothers that the pot would not fill. The brothers asked her to go a little further into the water. The sister went in further and even when she was in the waist deep water, the pot would not fill. The brothers asked her to go ahead. The sister went in a little further and the water was up to her neck. The *Bonga* who resided under the water pulled her inside. The brothers hastened home.

Some days later the body rose and floated to the bank and a bamboo clump sprang up. One day a *dome* (a low caste man) went to cut the bamboo clump to make a flute of it. When he raised his axe, somebody spoke to him, "O dome, please cut low down and don't cut high up." The dome was surprised, as he could not see anyone around. He however, obeyed the voice and cut the bamboo close to the ground. He made a flute of the bamboo. The flute produced beautiful music. Now the dome had a Santal boy as his great friend. The Santal boy pressed the dome that the flute should be given to him and the dome made a present of it to the Santal boy.

The Santal boy would not leave the flute even for a moment. He played on it almost the whole day and somehow the words flowed out of the tune: "I've come—I've come." The Santal boy was quite surprised at the music the flute produced. On the first night he slept with the flute by him. In the night the flute was changed into a beautiful girl and the girl told him as to how she had been disposed of. Every night the flute became a woman and in the early part of the morning she would go outside the house on some pretext and disappear. One night when she was about to disappear, the Santal seized her and forced her to stay with him till the sun came out. With the coming out of the sun, the girl could not disappear and retained her human form. The girl was called the flute-girl and she and the Santal were betrothed and soon afterwards got themselves married.

6

HARES & MEN

THE Santals are very fond of trapping and eating hares. But the Santals do not clean the hares they kill, but cook them entrails and all.

In the bygone days, however, it were the hares who used to eat men and men were scared of the hares. Men could see in the jungles tigers, deer and bisons coming and could fight and kill them. But the hares took the men unawares and would suddenly pounce on them and bite. In those days the hares had poisonous small teeth and their bite brought death to men.

The men held a council. It was decided that they should go and meet the *Thakur*, the God above and complain. So they went to the heaven and complained to the *Thakur* On hearing them the *Thakur* sent for the king of hares. The *Thakur* heard the king of hares but he asserted on the contrary that men ate hares. This was denied by the men.

Then *Thakur* said : "Oh hare and man, I have asked you both and you give different answers. Now, I order you, the king of hares to watch a *Kita* tree and if within a year you see a leaf fall from the tree, bring it up to me and I shall allow you to eat men; and you, man, shall watch a *Korkot* tree and if you see a leaf fall, then men will eat hares. The watch will begin from today and next year this day both of you, hare and man will bring me the leaves."

So the vigil started for both the hare and the men. They watched and watched but no leaf from either of the trees would fall. But just on the last day of the year, a *Korkot* leaf fell and the man was happy. He took it to *Thakur*. But what did the hare do ? As no leaf had fallen even at the last date, the hare bit off a leaf with its teeth and took it to the *Thakur*.

The *Thakur* examined the two leaves and found that the hare had brought a leaf which it had bitten off. The mark of the hare's teeth was there. The *Thakur* told the hare : "Look at the mark of your teeth. The tip of the stalk is quite different from the stalk of the leaf the man has brought." The hare put down his head in shame as he was caught. The *Thakur* decided that the hares shall not be able to eat men any longer. The *Thakur* rubbed the legs of the hare with a ball of cleaned cotton and told him, "Ah, you will be able to run very fast and try to save yourself from man: But if man should hunt you, he should kill and eat you, entrails and all."

From that day, the hares could no longer eat men and the men ate hares, entrails and all.

7

HOW LITA REVIVED HIS FATHER ?

LITA was the son of the *Handi Manjhi* of the village. A *Handi Manjhi* literally means a "liquor chief" and has to be elected if a Santal village has got a Headman of another race as a *Pradhan*. In that case, the Santals must have a *Handi Manjhi* who performs all the duties of a Santal village-chief except collecting rent and doing work required either by the government or the landlord.

Lita played beautifully on the flute. He would take cattle for grazing and play on his flute, to the extent that the cattle would stray into the jungle. He had a friend, Somra who was also a flute player. As Somra's father was an *ojha* (witch-doctor) and earned quite a bit of money, Somra had more leisure and would join Lita everyday and compete in playing on the flute. Lita's flute had six holes for stops and one for the blowing part of it. He himself had made the flute. But he had also purchased from a *dome* another one stringed fiddle with a hollow "breast", as they call it, covered with a piece of skin of a large *ajgar* snake (python). When playing this instrument Lita would keep it in front of him with the string turned away. His friend Somra being the son of an *ojha* had a different kind of stringed-instrument basides his flute. Somra's stringed-instrument included a hollow piece of a pumpkin covered at one end with a bit of skin through which a double string is run. He would keep the instrument in the left armpit and the left hand stretched the two strings with a small piece of wood tied to them. Now this type of a stringed-instrument is strictly confined to the disciples of an *ojha* and others cannot use it.

Now these two boys played on the flute and the other instruments the whole day and in their zeal forgot about the cattle which had strayed into the jungles. Towards the evening they would remember about the cattle and went into jungles to recover them. Once on their way back from the jungle they came across a very old woman with wrinkles all over and a bent body. This woman must have been at least 150 years of age. The woman stretched her hand for some alms. Lita and his friend Somra had caught different kinds of rats and some mushrooms and they offered them to the old woman. The old woman was happy and she blessed them. She suddenly disappeared but before she did so she told Lita to hurry back home as there was a mishap in his family. Before Lita could ask her as to what it was she had completely disappeared. Lita and Somra knew that she must have been a *Huty Budhi* (a supernatural very old woman). They hurried back to Lita's home and found that Lita's mother was in tears. Lita asked her as to what had happened and she told that while the *Handi Manjhi* had gone into the jungles to bring certain kinds of leaves and flowers for doing some ritual, a big rhinoceros had carried him off on his horn. A village party had gone inside the jungle but could not trace the rhinoceros or the body of the *Handi Manjhi*.

There were lamentations going on but Lita made up his mind to go into the jungle himself and see what has happened to his father. Somra also wanted to accompany him. Leaving their flutes and stringed musical intruments aside, the two boys made a selection of their arrows. They wanted to carry special arrows to shoot at the rhinoceros. They rejected the blunt arrow meant for shooting birds and tiny animals. They took iron-edged arrows and two battle axes. Lita's mother gave them two talismans of tiger's claws. She also gave them some rice and dried tubers, and some "barter oil". Barter oil is a mixed mustard oil used for cooking. The name is due to the fact that this kind of oil is in such great demand that it could always be bartered for anything else. The Santals in the olden days did not and could not have any business transactions among themselves or with outsiders. They created what they needed. They would make their own salt, cloth, weapons and utensils. When any one wanted a cow or a wife or something which they required badly, they were obtained by barter. Mustard oil was always handy for this barter.

Lita and his friend went into the jungle and walked through the whole night in moonlight. At about midnight they came to a hut inside the jungle. They were thoroughly tired and knocked at the door in search of a bed for the night. They were amazed to see that the door was opened by the same old *Huty Budhi* who had met them before. The old woman greeted them and asked them to come in and wanted straightaway the barter oil as she could not fry the rats and the mushrooms that had been given as she did not have any oil. Lita gave her the barter oil and she was pleased. After the cooking was over and they had eaten a good bit of the rats, mushrooms and rice, the old woman gave the direction where they would find the big rhinoceros. She told the boys that on the way they will meet tigers and other animals but they should not shoot at them. She particularly wanted them not to shoot any other rhinoceros except the giant one which had carried away Lita's father.

The two friends went on and on and saw cow-bisons, tigers and bears on their way. They did not give a second glance to these animals and the animals also passed by them without doing any harm. Various kind of birds, big and small, met them on the way. But the friends had no eyes for the birds or their beautiful plumage. Then they came to a shiny water-pool and they found that there were a number of rhinoceroses drinking water Lita and Somra waited for the giant rhinoceros with the body of Lita's father stuck to its horn to be separated from the other animals. After the animals had their fill, the giant rhinoceros that was the head of the group snorted and came out of the water pool and shook its head to indicate that the party shall now follow him. Lita did not lose the opportunity. Both the friends shot arrows after arrows from their iron-bows and the arrows went through the animals head. The giant rhinoceros turned a somersault and fell dead on the ground. The other rhinoceroses turned tail and ran away. The two boys went and pulled the dead-body of the *Handi Manjhi* off the horn of the dead animal. The body was laid down at the foot of a tree and both the boys began to weep over it. Lo, the *Huty Budhi* appeared once again out of the blue and told them : "Don't cry any more, take a cloth and wet it in the lake and then let your father's body be wrapped in it. Then whip the body with a *meral* twig and see what happens." So saying *Huty Budhi* suddenly disappeared. The boy obeyed her instructions faithfully and the dead man sat up alive. He rubbed his eyes and said : "I must have been sleeping for a long time. Where are the tubers and other leaves I'd gathered ?" Lita and Somra explained to him all that had happened and took him home.

There was a big feast to mark the return of

Handi Manjhi. Countless goats and pigs were killed and eaten. After the Santals had their fill of meat and drink they broke into dance and music. Lita and Somra were the main flute players while others beat the *madal* (drum), and the Santals damsels with bright flowers on their hair, danced and danced.

8

THE BONGA'S CAVE

THERE was a young *Bonga* who wanted to marry a woman. He dwelt in a cave in the Kachamkata jungle near a hill spring and a water-pool. Almost everyday he would notice village girls coming to the water pool and the spring for a bath. But as they were always in a group of five or six, he could not possibly catch hold of any. He wanted somehow to isolate a girl and take her to his cave and marry her.

The *Bonga* hit up on a plan. Everyday he placed on a flat stone outside his cave a pot of oil, a comb, a looking glass and some lamp-black or vermilion. By his magic the *Bonga* made these articles visible only to a woman. No man passing that way could see them.

The girls were attracted by these articles. They began to use the comb and looking glass and applied oil to their hair. They would go to the flat stone before collecting firewood or leaves or even before they had their bath.

One day five girls went to the jungle and together left the place after they had combed their hair. The *Bonga* had managed to steal a girl's bangle without the girl's knowing about it. By his magic again the *Bonga* made the girl realize at some distance that she had lost a bangle. She went back to recover the bangle and the *Bonga* immediately came out, threw his arms round her and dragged her to the cave. She shouted to her friends and they ran to her rescue but could only see her disappearing behind the cave. There was a big stone on the mouth of the cave and the girls could do nothing !

The girls took the news of the misfortune to the girl's parents. The parents came and sang a song in an attempt to make the girl come out. The girl sang back :

"Mother, I'm shut in a cave,
With a stone-door, he has shut me in,
Mother, you must go back home."

The parents went back disappointed.

But the *Bonga* treated her very well and after some time the girl was not unhappy. After some time she told her *Bonga* husband that it is only proper that they should pay a visit to her parents. The *Bonga* agreed and they took a big basket of sweet cakes and rice cooked with turmeric. The parents were very happy to see the girl once more and so were the younger brother and his wife.

The parents opened the big basket and found that it was filled up with cowdung cakes and bits of stone. The parents kept quiet but the girl insisted that they should eat the sweet cakes. Through the *Bonga's* magic, the *Bonga* wife saw cakes and rice while the parents saw only cowdung cakes and bits of stone. However, the parents avoided eating that bad stuff and decided that something must be done to kill the *Bonga* son-in-law.

There was a good feast followed by drinking

of home-brewn rice beer. The younger brother of the girl had mixed up some herbal medicine, in the drink which made the *Bonga* sleep very deeply. At mid-night the younger brother came with a hatchet made red hot under the fire and cut the *Bonga's* head off. The girl wept a little for some time but was happy later on.

9

THE BONGA HEADMAN

THIS is a true story where the villagers think that they have a *Bonga* Headman who lives on top of a banyan tree. Sarjomghutu is a village about four miles from Barhait Bazar on the banks of the Badi river. Barhait Bazar has a big weekly *hat* (fair) where grain is sold on the *hat* day. The villagers of Sarjomghutu found that any Headman (*Pradhan*) who was appointed invariably died. At Barhait Bazar a *sokha* (witch-doctor) used to come on the *hat*-days. After three such Headmen of Sarjomghutu had died, the villagers approached the *sokha* at Barhait Bazar to give them some help. After a good deal of recital of *mantras*, the *sokha* got into a trance. While in trance he started muttering : "I shall not allow any one else to become the *pradhan* of Sarjomghutu. I live at the top of the large banyan tree on the bank of the Badi river. The villagers of Sarjomghutu should obey me as the Headman." After the trance broke, the *sokha* told them that they should not elect any one else as the Headman as they had a *Bonga* as their Headman living at the top of the large banyan tree.

From this day the villagers got on very well with the *Bonga*. As a matter of fact, this *Bonga* at the top of the banyan tree, although unseen, would help the villagers in every possible way. If there was to be a wedding or a number of visitors would be coming to someone's house and there were not enough plates and dishes, the man went to the banyan tree and asked the Headman to lend him some. Then he goes back to his house. He goes again to the tree and finds a number of plates and dishes waiting for him there. After the feast he has to take back all the plates and dishes, well cleaned. The plates and dishes left there would disappear in no time.

The *Bonga* Headman insists on periodical sacrifices of goats and chickens. The story goes that the villagers in the bygone days even used to offer human sacrifices. But there has been no human sacrifice for the last fifty years.

The large shady banyan tree of Sarjomghutu village is still held in great veneration.

10

MARRIAGE WITH BONGAS

AS has been mentioned earlier, the Santals have a great belief in the world of the *Bongas* or spirits. Now there are both good and evil *Bongas*. Normally a *Bonga* is taken to be evil and to keep the *Bongas* in good humour the Santals offer sacrifices of fowls and goats. For particular types of *Bongas*, birds of a particular coloured feather have to be offered. For some *Bongas* a black fowl is to be given while for the others some pearl feathered birds are sacrificed.

Santal children are often threatened that if they stray away to far off villages or go to the interior of thick forests, *Bonga* girls will get hold of them and marry them. The Santal boys grow up in this belief.

In a small village called Darbar, which is close to the huge Silingi village—a very large one, two friends lived. One of them was very fond of playing on the flute while tending the cows. He was an expert flute player and his playing attracted a *Bonga* female who took shape of a girl and came to him. After they became friends for some time, she invited him to visit her parents and said that if her parents approve she would immediately marry him. The boy agreed and the *Bonga* female led him to a hut in the interior of the forest. As soon as the boy entered the hut he realized where he was. He found that the seats in the hut were coiled up snakes and in the cow shed a number of tigers and leopards lived. The boy wanted to go away but the girl insisted on his staying for dinner. They had a meal of dried rice, curd and *gur* (molasses). The boy was given a good quantity of dried rice and rice cakes to take home. The boy promised to come back the next day. When the boy reached his house, he sent for his friend who knew about his intimacy with the girl. When the friend came they opened the bundle to eat the sweet cakes and rice but they found there were only cowdung cakes and bits of stone. The friend immediately knew that his friend was in the clutches of the *Bonga* female.

But the attraction of the *Bonga* female was far too strong to be diminished by theis revelation. The boy saw her again the next day. He started visiting her frequently. A marriage, unknown to the Santals, was performed. The *Bonga* girl saw to it that her lover's flocks and herds increased and he became rich.

But the boy's father was extremely unhappy on his own son's having married a *Bonga* girl. He went to witch-doctor in the Silingi village. This *sokha* (witch-doctor), however, told him that his powers were limited and he should go to another witch-doctor at Mahesmunda village who knew how to drive away the influence of the *Bonga* girl. The father went to the *sokha* in Mahesmunda village. The *sokha* asked the man to see him again on the following Tuesday with his son and four black fowls with a tuft of white feather somewhere on the body. With a great deal of search, the father procured four fowls. The following Tuesday he went to the *sokha* with his son. The *sokha* performed certain rituals and recited some incantations and sacrificed the birds one after the other. The *sokha* kept back three of the birds and gave one of the slaughtered birds to the father to be cooked and eaten by both the father and the son. After this ritual was done, the boy never saw the *Bonga* girl again.

Silingi and Darbar villages are still there in the District of Santal Parganas in Bihar.

11

THE TWO BROTHERS AND THE PANCHAYAT

THE advice of village elders is often sought in the Santal Parganas as in some other areas of the country to settle family disputes This institution is known as the Panchayat as originally *panch* or five people would sit together and decide the quarrel. The Panchayat system still exists although not much in use now. Villagers have learnt to take their disputes to the court.

There were two brothers who used to fall out for every little thing and were constantly quarrelling. They would. quarrel even as to who should plough the field and who should do the grazing of the cattle. One day they had a heated quarrel over a petty matter. The younger brother quickly asked the village Headman to bring the Panchayat to his house the next morning and decide the matter. The Panchayat agreed.

Next day at dawn the younger brother had become quite calm and when his elder brother visited him and told him that he has to share the expense for the purchase of a goat to give a feast to the Panchayat that he had called, the younger brother started regretting his action. It is usual that after the Panchayat gives a decision there will be a feast with meat and home-brewn liquor. The younger brother told the elder brother : "Brother, I am sorry I called the villagers. The Panchayat is sure to fine us both and at the top of it all we have to give them the feast. It is all my foolishness and let us do something to get out if it." The elder brother said : "My dear brother, now that you have realized the folly of taking our quarrels to others. I hope you will also realize that we should stop our endless quarrels. If we must have them, let us keep them to ourselves—it is no use making a fool of ourselves by taking our quarrels to others."

Both the brothers agreed that henceforth they will behave better. But what should be done now ? They pondered over the question again and again. How to avoid the Panchayat and the purchase of a goat and the cooking of a good quantity of rice ?

The older one advised : "Look, when they come and ask you as to what was the cause of the quarrel, you just say that it is for them to find out. And there will be no party if they fail to find out the reason."

The idea was to give this foolish reply which will irritate the Panchayat which will disperse without the feast.

When the villagers came and asked what the quarrel was about, the younger brother said : "Don't you know why the quarrel ? That was the very matter I wanted you to decide. How can you judge about if you don't know it ? If I give you the cause I will give my own version and you'll be prejudiced. So I'm not going to tell you anything."

The villagers turned to the other brother and asked him what the reason was. The elder brother said that he did not know as to why the younger brother had given them the trouble. The Panchayat repeated the question to the younger brother and the younger brother again and again came out with the same silly answar. The villagers were very angry and said that their time had been wasted and the two brothers must give them dinner. The brothers flatly declined to give any dinner as no decision had been given and pointed out that unless a decision is given the Panchayat cannot claim a dinner. The Head of the Panchayat nodded his head and the Panchayat went away grumbling. The two brothers shook each other's hand on having scored a victory and saved the money.

Henceforth, the two Santal brothers lived in peace and amity.

12

THE DOG BRIDE

A young boy used to collect the cattle of the village and took them to the grazing ground. While watching the animals he noticed that every noon a bitch used to come and go into the Sal jungle* nearby. After some time the bitch returned.

The cowherd boy was curious to find out as to why the bitch went to the forest almost at the same time every day. One noon he followed the bitch and hid himself when the bitch went near a tank. To his great surprise, he found that the bitch shed its dog-skin and took the form of a beautiful maiden and began to bathe. After her bath, she put on her skin, became a bitch again and went to the village. The boy followed her and watched the house in which the bitch went.

After watching the bitch do the same again and again, the boy went to a sooth-sayer in a distant village and gave him the details. The sooth-sayer told the young man that the bitch was really a human being but for some bad deeds in her past life had to lead the life of a bitch. But if anyone can burn the dog-skin when it is shed, she would

* Sal forests are very common in Santal Parganas. Sal is Soria robusta. The Santals hold the trees in great veneration.

continue to be a human being. The boy did not give out the details to anyone.

The parents of the cowherd boy had already started looking for a suitable bride. The boy told his mother that he would only take a bitch as his bride. The parents laughed and thought that the boy was off his head. But the boy persisted and the parents had to yield.

When the proposal was made, the bitch's master laughed. He was, however, a greedy man and when he was told that he would be given one buffalo and one cow as the bride price,* he agreed to the marriage.

On an auspicious day, the bridegroom party went to the house of the bitch's master. The marriage ceremony was gone through. According to the custom the bridegoom put *Sindur* (vermilion)** on the forehead of the bitch.

Next morning the party returned to the house of the bridegroom. Before the ceremonial mid-day meal was served, bride slipped out and the boy knew that she was going for her bath. He followed the bitch but kept himself away so that he was not seen. As usual, the bitch cast off its dog-skin and a beautiful girl came out and got into the pond for her bath. The boy came out from the hiding and immediately put fire to the dog-skin and burnt it.

* Among the Santals, it is customary to give a bride price to the bride's parents. Usually it consists of some cattle and grain.

In marriage, putting of *Sindur* on the forehead of the bride is an important ritual. Even if a Santal boy forcibly puts *Sindur* on an unmarried girl, the girl will have to be his bride. Very often in a *hat* a Santal boy pounces on a girl (usually this is prearranged) and puts vermilion and runs away. After that the parents have got to meet and mutually fix the bride price and perform the marriage.

The girl screamed when she found that the dog-skin was burnt. But she was happy to go back with the boy as his bride.

Everyone was wonder-struck to see the pair coming back smiling. The boy gave out the story and every-one was very pleased. The cowherd boy and his wife lived happily everafter.

13

LITA AND HIS ANIMALS

AT Patsunda village in Godda sub-division of Santal Parganas there lived a Santal family. Lita was the youngest member of the family. His other three brothers were married and lived in the same house with their wives. The atmosphere in the house was hardly cordial as there was constant tiff between the wives and the in-laws. The first brother had married according to *Kiring-bahu* system of Santal marriage which means a daughter-in-law is bought. The second brother was more adventurous and he had married according to the *Itut* system. *Itut* means paint-smearing. The boy puts some red paint on the forehead of a girl whom he loves, as and when he gets an opportunity. The second bride was rather haughty in temperament and thought much of her. Peculiarly enough, the third bride came to the house and forced herself on the third brother as she had developed a liking for him after watching a good deal of him in the market and in the *akhras* (dancing place). This system of marriage is called *Nir-bolok*. The girl and the boy fell in love with each other but the boy started hesitating when the girl was with a child. So the girl forcibly entered the house and sat in a corner while the boy's mother tried to drive her out by burning tabacco leaves and make her inhale the pungent smoke. She did not budge and ultimately the marriage had to be arranged, of course after giving a double feast to the villagers, according to the custom.

As there used to be constant quarrels in the house, Lita got disgusted and wanted to go out of the village to do some business.

Lita wanted his father to give him some money. The father agreed but asked Lita to wait till the *Baha Parab* was held. *Baha Parab* is a great festival among the Santals and naturally the parents wanted Lita to stay back for this festival. This festival takes place when the *Sal* trees begin to flower, usually in the month of February-March. The young people of the village observe the festival with great joy and the whole night is spent in drumming. An arrow is shot into a *Sal* tree in bloom Sacrifices of fowls, bunch of flowers and pigs are made.

After the festival Lita took sixty rupees from his father and left the village. He promised that if he lost the money he would not ask for his share in the paternal property. Lita did not exactly know where to go. After he had walked about fifteen miles, he came to a village where he was not known. He found that the villagers were chasing a cat in great excitement. He enquired and was told that the cat always spoilt the king's milk and the king had offered a reward of Rs 20 for anyone who killed it. Lita made an astonishing offer. He said he was willing to buy the cat for Rs 20 and to leave the village with it. So Lita bought the cat while the villagers also got the reward from the king and spent the money in feast.

Lita walked along and reached another village only to find the villagers hunting for an otter who would destroy the king's fish in a tank. Lita offered to buy the otter if he got it alive. He bought the otter for another Rs 20 and proceeded on his journey.

He put both the otter and the cat in the bag he was carrying along. He reached another village where he found the villagers running after a wild mouse with sticks. He discovered that the mouse would gnaw the king's papers and the king wanted it to be killed. Lita once again bought the mouse for the remaining Rs 20. He was happy with the animals he had bought. When he reached another village he found the villagers looking for a snake which had caused death to many villagers. Lita knew a *mantra* (incantation) by which he could snare the snake. He offered to catch the snake and take it away. The villagers agreed and Lita got the snake without paying any money.

Lita continued his journey. The snake told him : "Lita, if you had not come, I would have been killed. You come to my house and meet my parents. We are rich and I'll give anything you ask for. You have saved my life." At first Lita was afraid but the snake assured him that he or his parents will not be so ungrateful as to bite him. Lita visited the snake's house and the sanke's parents presented Lita with a ring which would produce anything he asked for. But the ring had to be first put in a glass of milk. Lita was happy. He went back home with the ring and the animal.

His parents were happy that Lita had come back home and did not question him as to how he spent the money. The brothers and their wives jeered at him that he had come back with three animals. Lita kept quiet and said that one day he would show what treasure he has got.

The parents were anxious that Lita should marry. They had chosen a bride who was rich and beautiful. But the girl had a great liking for another boy and wanted to avoid a marriage with Lita. She proposed that if the bridegroom would build a covered passage from her house to his and she could walk to a new home in shade she would marry. Lita's parents were taken aback and wanted to break off the negotiations. Lita, however, told his parents to go ahead with the marriage and that he would see to the making of a covered passage. The parents thought that Lita must have come back with a good deal of money he has kept concealed somewhere. The negotiations were finalised. A day before the marriage Lita's parents and brothers were very anxious as they saw that Lita was doing nothing about the covered passage and was going about with his flute or bow and arrows. They took Lita to task and said they were going to be put to great humiliation as the covered passage was not built and the marriage would break off. Lita retired to a lonely spot with a pale of milk and put his ring in the milk and wanted that the covered passage be built. To the surprise of everyone the covered passage was automatically built and the marriage took place.

The bride came to Lita's place and wanted Lita to tell her how the covered passage could be built in a few minutes. Lita did not tell her. The bride asked the mother-in-law and she said she knew nothing of the matter. Lita's wife was still meeting the young boy she had fallen in love with and they planned to escape together. Lita's wife asked her lover to wait till she could get from Lita the secret of making the covered passage within a few moments.

Lita's wife became very sullen and for every little thing would tell Lita that he was keeping back the secret of the covered passage from her and that shows that he did not love her. At last Lita told her about the ring. Lita's wife quickly informed her lover that they must run away that very night and that he should kill a goat and bring the blood of the goat in an earthen pot. In the night when Lita was asleep, she took the ring from his finger and poured all the blood of the goat on the ground under the bed on which Lita was sleeping. Lita's wife and the boy ran away. Next morning Lita missed his wife. The family saw the pool of blood under the bed. The villagers also came to know about it. There was a natural suspicion that Lita had killed his wife. The wife's parents who lived in another part of the village came running to Lita's house and started howling and called for justice. The village Headman and Chowkidar came and reported the matter to the Magistrate. Lita was arrested and put in jail.

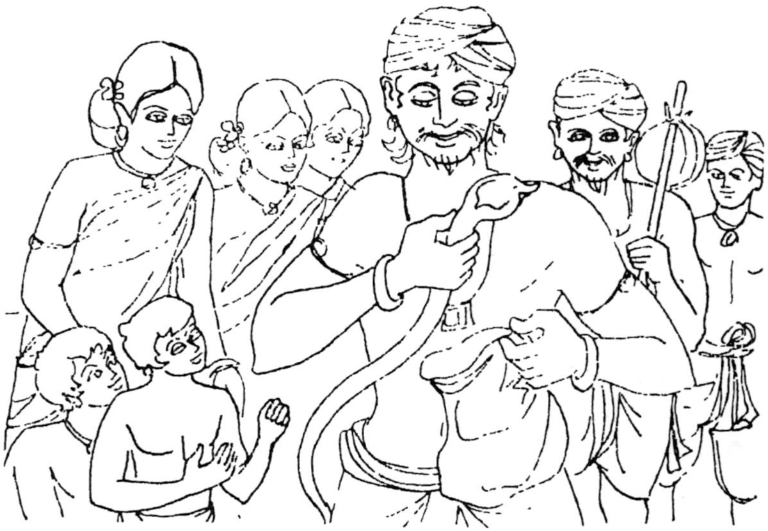

It, however, came out the next day that the lover of Lita's wife was also missing. Lita had already protested his innocence and the Magistrate also thought that Lita's wife had actually run away with her lover and that she was not murdered. Lita had the animals with him. He told the animals that if the ring could be recovered he would be able to prove his innocence.

The animals started searching and found Lita's wife and her lover in a lonely village. They were very careful and used to fasten and bolt every entrance very squarely so that no one could get admittance. The cat and the otter told the mouse that he must collect all the mice in the neighbourhood and they must burrow through the wall and find some means of recovering the magic ring.

The mouse collected hundreds of his tribe and bored a hole through the wall. The animals entered the house and started searching for the ring. The fingers and toes of the two were searched but the ring was not there. The clothes were examined. But the ring was not there either. One clever rat thought that the woman might have kept the ring in her mouth. The rat tickled her nose with the tip of its tail. This made her sneeze and the ring came out. The ring was actually hidden in her mouth. The mouse seized the ring and ran out. The party of Lita's animals came back to the prison where Lita had been put and gave him the ring.

Lita asked for a pale of milk. The ring was put in the pale of milk and Lita wanted the ring to bring the bed on which his faithless wife and her lover were sleeping that very night. The bed was actually brought to the prison and everyone saw that Lita's wife was alive. The lover of Lita's wife was heavily fined and had to pay Lita double the expenditure which had been incurred on his marriage. The marriage was dissolved.

Lita's parents got another wife for him. This girl was good and they lived happily. Lita's animals wanted to be released and Lita took the otter to a tank which was full of fish and put the otter in the tank. He took the cat and mouse to a big bazar and let both of them free. That was the last he saw of his animals.

14

THE BRIDE THAT FAILED

A party of four men went to a Santal's house to see if a particular girl would make a suitable bride for the son of one of their friends. It is usual among the Santals to go and see girls in this way. While they were talking to the girl, another young girl came up. The visitors asked the first girl where her father was and she replied : "My father has gone to meet water." The answer was a puzzle but the group did not want to show that they could not follow her. They asked the girl where her mother was and she replied : "My mother has gone out to make two men out of one." This was all the more puzzling. At this moment, the other girl got up and left the place saying : "While I have been waiting here, I could have carded a seer of cotton."* The group of men was highly impressed with the remark of the second girl as they thought she must be very industrious and was much better than the other girl who gave puzzling answers. They found out the second girl's parents and returned home after fixing up the match between the second girl and the friend's son.

On their return home the men told their wives as to what they have done. The wives laughed and said that the answers of the first girl were very

*Carding and spinning were quite common in the villages of Santal Parganas. Even now there are expert Santal weavers in some villages. There are some villages where very good silk fabric is made.

clever. The wives explained that what she meant was that her father had gone to reap thatched grass and her mother had gone to thresh dal.

However, the marriage took place. It was found that the girl only wanted to impress the group and she knew nothing of carding cotton or spinning thread. When her mother-in-law questioned her closely as to why she had made that remark when she did not know how to card, she replied : "Oh, I can card and spin but only with the spinning wheel at my father's place. But that was also a ruse. Her father-in-law got the spinning wheel from her parents' house and she could not spin. She was found to be a very dull girl and the boy's father blamed his four friends for recommending an inefficient bride.

15

HOW A TIGER WAS KILLED

WHEN jungle patches are cultivated and crops grow, the man who cultivates has to watch the crops at night lest the crops are destroyed by the cattle or used by the thieves. Once a Santal went to watch his crop from the platform that he had put up in his field. Usually these platforms are built on a tree that is available near the field or, if no tree is available, thick bamboos are fixed in the ground and a platform is built.

While going to the field to watch the crops, the Santal found a goat and killed it. He took it to maize patch with some fire-wood, a knife and a hatchet. He hoisted them all to his platform and lit fire below an earthen pot. He sliced the animal and started cooking it. A tiger, having smelt the flesh, came and adjusted itself under the platform.

As he ate, he threw the bones away simultaneously. The tiger did not let the bones fall on the ground and caught them mid-air. After some time the man realized that he did not hear the bones fall. He was curious. To his horror he found the tiger leaping at the bones.

He, however, retained his senses and continued to throw bones with bits of meat to the tiger. Then he put the top of the hatchet in fire and when it became red hot, he threw that too. The tiger leapt and gulped the iron piece and then, in severe pain, roared around. The tiger's tongue and palate burnt and he ran only to slump to the ground at some distance.

Next morning the man stepped down the platform and received a hero's welcome in the village. The tiger was cut into pieces which were distributed amongst the villagers. The tiger's fat, claws and whiskers are valued for their power to produce medicines for various diseases.

16

THE PRINCE WHO BECAME THE KING OF THE JACKALS

SANTALS believe in *Bongas* (spirits) and think that the *Bongas* are always either being helpful or creating some mischief. If there is a cattle epidemic and cattle die, the Santals think that certain *Bongas* are unhappy with them and need to be pleased. They make sacrifices of fowls and their priests repeat *Mantras* to satisfy the *Bongas*.

Once upon a time when the land of Santal Parganas had a large number of small kings and kingdoms, one of the kings' son was very friendly with a barber. The king was not very happy and in one of his furious moods he ordered his son to quit the kingdom. The prince left the royal palace with his friend and after travelling a long distance reached a village where nobody knew them. At that particular moment they both were penniless and looked around for work. The barber started a school for children and the prince took up a job with a *Mahajan* (Moneylender). The *Mahajan* clearly told the prince that as his wages, the prince would get a plate of rice and some *sag* but if he (the prince) left the job on his own, he would be deprived of a piece of his skin. The prince agreed to the rigid terms but soon he realized that it was impossible to carry on. The leaf plate became smaller and smaller and the quantity of rice was also reduced proportionately. One day in a fit of fury and depression he told the moneylender that he could not carry on with such meagre ration and as such was giving up the job. The moneylender permitted him to go but not without chopping off a piece of his skin. The prince felt embarrassed and explained the situation to his friend who consoled him. They decided to take a revenge.

Next day the barber went to the moneylender and offered his services. The moneylender insisted on the same terms. The barber agreed but on the condition that if he was dismissed by the moneylender, the latter will also have to give a piece of his skin. The moneylender agreed. The barber started vexing the moneylender and would deliberately neglect his job and do it indifferently. If he was asked to bring a handful of *sag* from the field, the barber would bring all of it from the field, thus causing considerable damage to the moneylender. And when asked to cook rice, he would cook it badly and break the earthen pot in which rice was cooked. Having been disgusted with the barber's ways, the moneylender dismissed him. The barber left the place after chopping off a piece of the moneylender's skin.

The prince and the barber decided that they should leave the village and find a place elsewhere. They went on and on and reached the land of the jackals. They wanted to know where the king of the jackals lived. They were told that the king lived in a cave, under a big *Sal* tree. They both went to the jackal king and found him sleeping outside the cave. The barber quickly shaved off the hair on the jackal's tail and then they both hid themselves nearby. When the jackal woke up and found its hair shaved, the jackal thought that it must have been done by the *Bongas*. He thought of a bigger danger which might be forthcoming. So he ran away and came across a bear on the way who naturally asked him the reason of his running away. The jackal apprised the bear of the situation. The bear consoled the jackal and agreed to go with him to drive away the *Bongas* with some incantations. They found a cart blocking the entrance to the cave. The bear had brought a white fowl for sacrifice. He rode the cart in order to perform the sacrifice. The barber immediately got hold of the bear's tail and the prince stabbed it with a knife. The bear did its best to get free but failed. Finding that the *Bongas* had taken complete hold of the bear, the jackal once again ran away. On the way the jackal came across a tiger. The tiger accompanied the jackal and was meted with similar treatment. As a last resort the jackal thought of sacrificing the white fowl to please the *Bongas*. In the process both the jackal and the white fowl got killed. All other jackals mourned the death of their king. At this moment the prince and the barber came out of the cave and told the assembly that they had been sent by the *Bongas* to take place of their king. The jackals agreed and from then the prince and the barber divided the jackals' kingdom into two halves and ruled over them.

17

THE MOUSE HUSBAND

IN Santal Parganas '*Sindur-Dan*' (putting of vermilion on the forehead of the girl) completes a marriage. There are cases where a Santal boy will forcibly put Sindur on the forehead of a girl either in the *hat* (market) or while she would be going to fetch water and run away. In such cases the girl's parents will pursue the boy and approach the parents of the boy who will have to complete the marriage by paying the bride price.

This is a story of a clever mouse who had planted some jute plants by the side of the path leading to the forest. The village girls while going to the forest to collect firewood and roots would pluck the flowers of the jute plants. The mouse would come out of the hole and rebuke them. The girls would laugh at it and continue to do so. One day the mouse was very angry and shouted : "If you go on plucking my flowers I will put *Sindur* on the forehead of one of you who will have to marry me." The girls laughed at the mouse. They never paid any attention to the mouse and would pluck the flowers every day. The mouse was very angry and brought some vermilion and concealed it in his hole. Next morning when the girls were plucking the jute flowers the mouse got on the body of a girl and put vermilion on her head. As has been mentioned, putting on vermilion or *Sindur-Dan* means marriage. The girl began to sob but she had no other alternative but to stay back. The mouse danced with joy and asked her to accompany him to his hole. The girl had to do so. The girl, however, could not get inside the hole and stayed out side. The mouse again started dancing and told the girl that if she cannot get into the hole she can remain outside but she will have to cook and feed him every day. The girl brought some water and began boiling rice. When the rice was boiled the mouse was very hungry and started dancing and asked the girl to pour out the *Phen* (rice gruel) in a pot so that he could drink a part of it. The girl did as she was asked to do and began to cook the *sag*-curry. The mouse was very happy and was dancing all the while that he had been able to win over the girl but while dancing madly in joy he fell into the pot where the hot rice gruel was kept and was drowned. The girl was released and took the curry and rice home and told her parents as to what had happened. The parents had to give a small feast where plenty of *hanria* (home brewn rice beer) was served and the village elders took back the girl into their fold.

18

THE HUSBAND WHO WAS AN OGRE

IT is commonly believed by the Santals that the soul in the body often goes out, takes another shape, mostly of animals and after doing mischief comes back quietly and gets into the body. The Santals think that many of the dreams are due to the fact that the soul has gone out of the body and the glimpses of what happens at that time come to the mind in the shape of dreams. This is a story of a husband who was really an ogre in the shape of a man.

In the good old days there lived a rich man who was a drunkard. His wife had to suffer because of this. She had to do all the household work and also look after him. The man did not even know his own son and was hardly in his senses. One day his wife played a trick on him. She made the servants and the son sit in a line and asked the husband when he was slightly sober to point out his own son. The man failed to do so. As a result the servants and the wife broke into a huge laughter. This embarrassed the man a lot. This shock amounted to his giving up drinking altogether.

The wife asked the husband to search a bride for their son. The man left his village in search of a girl.

On the way the man plucked a bright red *Gunja* flower. He also took a *Thaili* (small cloth bag) of money which he carefully concealed in his clothes. The man went on and on, visiting villages and usually stopped by the side of the village *Chuan* (water spring) where the village girls would come to draw water. At last he came to a village where he found a very beautiful girl drawing water from the *Chuan* and followed her. The girl was very fair and looked like the bright *Gunja* flower he had plucked. The man followed the girl and sat down near her house. He made acquaintance with the girl's parents who would not, however, take an interest in the man and thought he was a beggar. When the man disclosed that he was on the look out for a good girl to marry his son with, the Parents of the girl laughed and told him : "Have you got the money to give the bride price?" In Santal Parganas usually the bridegroom's party has to pay fees for getting a girl in their family. The man said : "What is your demand ?" The father of the girl replied : "We want one cow and six fowls and a bag of paddy. Can you give that?" The boy's father smiled and pulled out his *Thaili* and counted out the money for buying all that. The parents were impressed and gave him water to wash his feet and this was followed by a hearty meal and plenty of *hanria* (home-brewn rice beer). The marriage was settled. Unfortunately, on his way back and while going through a thick jungle, the man was attacked by a tiger and killed. After waiting for some time, the parents of the girl sent word to the boy and his mother that the dowry had already been paid and so the marriage should be solemnised. The boy came to the village on an auspicious day with a few elders and friends and the marriage was duly performed.

The girl was taken to the house of the boy. Very soon the girl found out that her husband's body would lie inert on the bed for sometime, almost every night. In spite of her speaking to him and giving him a push he would not stir. The fact was that the boy was an ogre and his soul would slip out in the night, take an ogre's shape and go about eating wild animals and even human beings. One night the young bride lay quietly and watched her husband. The boy got up and brought out a small stick from a *Jhampi* (basket) and touched himself with one end of the rod. He at once became ferocious and took the form of an ogre. Within moments he left the room. The wife was aghast. She, however, did not sleep and waited to see what happens. At dawn she saw the ogre come back and touch himself with the other end of the stick. The ogre at once took a human shape and actually slipped into the bed. The next morning when the husband went out with the cattle, the girl broke the rod and burnt it to ashes. That very night the wife again kept awake although pretending to be asleep. At dead of the night the boy got up and looked into the *Jhampi* for the rod but he did not find it. The wife got up and very gently told him that she had burnt the rod and that he should not continue to be an ogre but be a normal human being. At first the young husband was upset but the gentle words of the wife brought him around and he agreed. Since then the husband lived as a normal man and both of them continued to live very happily.

19

THE SACRIFICE

THERE were seven Santal brothers who all lived together with their wives. The Santals are very simple people. The brothers would take the cattle to the field every morning and also plough the little land they had. The wives would take their meals to the place of work.

For some reason the brothers had made a promise to the *Singbonga* (Supreme Deity) that they would sacrifice a goat. They brought a goat from the village *hat* (weekly market) and fixed a date for the sacrifice with the consent of the village priest. But it so happened that on the eve of the day of sacrifice the king's guard came and took away all the seven brothers to the royal court, saying that they had defaulted to pay their share of rent for the ploughs and the king wanted to punish them for this.*

Their wives were very upset. Before the brothers left they told the women that the sacrifice fixed must be performed, otherwise there will be greater misfortune.

Next morning the wives took out the goat, bathed it, anointed it with oil and put *sindur* (vermilion) on the forehead. Although they had known that it had to be done, but the problem was who would conduct the sacrifice ? The other wives told the *barki* (the eldest brother's wife) that she must do it as she was now the head of the family. The *barki* agreed.

---

* Originally rent was assessed on the number of ploughs a family had.

But there was another problem. The *babkri* took up the sacrificial knife and wanted to know as to which part of the goat had to be chopped off as she did not want to hurt the goat needlessly. She asked the other woman.

At first no one could give an answer. Then the *chutki* (the youngest brother's wife) said : "Let us watch and see what part of the goat moves as I have heard that life is never still. If any particular part moves, life lives there and that part must be struck." The wives now began to watch curiously when suddenly the goat moved its tail. "That's where its life is", shouted all the seven wives. Three or four of them caught hold of the goat's neck and the *barki* raised the knife and gave several cuts at the root of the goat's tail. The goat wriggled out in pain and ran away. The women followed it as they wanted to kill the goat outright and to eat the meat after offering the share to the Deity. The goat ran through a field of cotton and knocked off many of the ripe cotton pods. The women thought the pods were lumps of fat fallen from the wounded goat, so they took them home. As the goat escaped to the hill they could not catch hold of it.

As they were cooking the cotton pods and the goat's tail the husbands returned from the royal court after promising the king that the sacrificed goat would be brought to him as a penalty. The brothers wanted to know where the goat was and heard the story from their wives. They laughed at the foolishness of the women and told them that the goat bleats first and then moves the tail and so the life of the goat is in the motuh and the head needs to be chopped off first. When they found that cotton pods were being cooked, they laughed all the more. The brothers went out to the hills and managed to catch hold of the tail-less goat. The goat was killed and taken to the king after the *Singbonga's* share had been offered.

20

THE LAZY WIFE

A young Santal was married and he lived very happily with his wife. But soon he found that the wife was very lazy. Whenever work in the field was at its height and the man wanted the wife to work along with him, she would pretend to be ill. She would not even go to the hill-stream and bring water if the village wells dried up. She would complain of pain in her legs. At the same time, the husband found that she used to cook rice for herself when he was away and did not keep sufficient rice for him.

As the Santal youth was being constantly told by the wife that she was not keeping well, he thought some evil spirit had taken possession of her and he must consult an *ojha* (witch-doctor). Without telling his wife, the Santal approached an *ojha* who was known to be very powerful. Next morning the *ojha* came to the Santal's house and saw the young wife. He put certain questions to the girl and soon found out that she had no illness. The *ojha* told the husband that the malady was very serious and he will need one day to repeat his *mantras* (incantations) to find out which witch has caught hold of the woman.

The *ojha* had made up his mind as to what he

should do. He went to the jungle and dug up two large tubers of the *tirra* plant as big as pumpkins but kept them in the jungle. The *ojha* sent word that he has found the medicine after fixing the particular witch. He would visit the Santal's house at dawn the next morning and that a few young villagers should be collected. Next morning the *ojha* came after he had his bath. At the Santal's house, he repeated some unintelligible words and then, as if in trance, he started moving and asked the village youths along with Santal and his wife to follow. He took them to the jungle where the two large tubers had been kept. The *ojha* made the patient sit on the winnowing fan facing the east and painted her with vermilion. He asked for some pig's dung which was readily brought. He poured a quantity of pig's dung round her head and then pointed out the two tubers as the medicine for her serious illness. The two tubers were tied to her neck and the *ojha* told her to walk up and down the village street three times with the tubers on and that would remove the spell of the witch that was on her. The poor girl wanted to tell them that she suffered from no illness but could not possibly do that as that would have exposed her. The girl had to walk up and down the village street with two large tubers hanging round her neck and everyone laughed at her. The children were all jumping and shouting as they thought it was great fun. The *ojha* followed shouting. "You must not remove the tubers until you are fully cured. The moment you are cured, you will yourself remove them. You will not find it difficult to work hard in the fields and bring water from the stream. You will also not eat more than your husband." The girl took the hint, and after she had done the village path twice, she took off the tubers and ran home. The husband and the *ojha* followed her with others. She was asked if she was cured. The woman only smiled in reply. The *ojha* warned her to take care because if she was again caught under the spell, he would have to apply the same remedy.

From that day the Santal woman did her full and fair share of all the works.

21

THE GOALA AND THE COW

THE Goala caste has the occupation of tending cows, graze them and sell the milk and milk-products. They are sturdy people. It is said that at first Goalas were not very careful in treating their cattle. The following is the story widely prevalent in Santal Parganas and it is said that because of this story men of the Goala caste now treat their cattle well.

Long time ago a Goala boy was going for his marriage. He was seated in a *palki* (palanquin) and was followed by a number of friends. While the bridegroom was passing by a pool of water, he heard a voice saying : "Please stop, happy bridegroom, for a while; spare a thought for my misfortune and pull me out of this quagmire." The bridegroom found that a cow had stuck fast in the mud at one side of the pool. The bridegroom refused to help as he was afraid his clothes would become muddy. He spoke to the cow rather harshly, "I cannot help you, I am in a hurry."

The cow cursed that Goala, saying : "You did not help me because you thought your clothes would become muddy. I curse you—the moment you touch your bride, you shall turn into a donkey." The Goala bridegroom took the curse casually and went along. But the cow was not absolutely cruel. While the Goala was going away, the cow told him, "Look, although I have cursed you, it would be possible for your wife to restore you to human shape." The bridegroom did not pay any attention to this part of the curse as well.

While the marriage was being performed, the Goala had to put vermilion on the bride's forehead. As soon as he touched the bride with his finger, he became a donkey. The bride's parents were aghast and wanted to beat the donkey and drive it away. But the bride said that as *Thakur* (God) for some reason has given her a donkey husband, she would cling to him. The bridegroom's party returned downcast with shame and anguish but the bride stuck to her donkey husband. As everyone laughed at her in the bridegroom's village, she thought she would run away to some other country where nobody knew her. Without telling anyone, she packed up some provisions for the journey and set out with the donkey.

The young girl walked on and on till she arrived at a tank with a large well near it. It was mid-day and the sun was hot. She wanted a little rest. She turned the donkey loose to graze on the banks of the tank and sat down by the well to eat some of the food she had brought with her. In the field, below the tank, about twenty plough-men of the local king were working to make the fields ready for the sowing of seeds. It got past noon but no one brought food for the labourers and they began to grumble. At last a maid-servant of the king came with food in a basket on her head and with her child following her. The maid-servant put the basket of food near the plough-men and then went off to the well to draw some water for them. The child followed the mother.

Just at this moment, a marriage procession passed along the road with the beating of the drums and music. The maid-servant had her eyes fixed on the procession while she took the rope for tying the neck of the big water-pot to pull out water. Without knowing it, she tied the rope round the neck of her own child and lowered him into the well. While still gazing at the procession and admiring the music, she pulled up the rope, and then to her horror, found that the child was dead. She was not only very upset but also afraid as to what her husband and other people in the family would say. She lost her child and stood the risk of being taken to task as the murderer of the child. She thought of a plan.

She took the dead child in her arms and ran to the king. She complained that as she was a little late in taking food to the plough-men, they had beaten her child to death. She added that a woman was sitting by the well and grazing a donkey and she must have seen all that had passed.

The king at once sent a guard to bring the plough-men. The plough-men came and spoke the truth but the woman still denied. The king asked the men if they could produce any witness that the child had been put in the well by mistake and had died. The plough-men also mentioned that there was a woman sitting by the well and grazing her donkey. The king sent for the woman. The woman could not leave the donkey behind but took the donkey along with her and went to the king's court. The guards asked her to leave the donkey outside the palace. She replied that if she had to go, the donkey must also go. The guards then allowed her to take the donkey along with her.

The king was surprised that the strange woman came along with her donkey. She also told the king that the donkey could not be separated even for a moment. However, the king asked her if she had seen anything. Truthfully, she mentioned as to what had happened. The maid-servant still stuck to her story. The king asked the Goala girl to take a solemn oath. The Goala-bride replied that she was ready to take an oath and swear by the donkey. If she spoke the truth, the donkey would turn into a man and if she lied it would remain a donkey. The king was amazed. He, however, said: "If you take oath, the case shall be decided accordingly. You are a strange woman." The Goala-bride repeated what she had seen and then making *johar* (obeisance) to *Chando* (a deity) she said: "*Chando*, punish me if I have lied but if I have spoken the truth, may this ass become a man."

Uttering this oath, she laid her hand on the back of the donkey. It at once resumed its human shape.

The case was decided accordingly. The maid-servant was punished for trying to establish a false charge against the plough-men and was turned out of the king's court. The king was very pleased with the

Goala-bride and her husband. He gave them enough riches and a nice house to live in. He also gave them one hundred cows.

From that time, men of the Goala caste have always been very careful to treat their cattle well.

22

LAKHAN AND THE WILD BUFFALOES

LAKHAN and his widow-mother lived a very frugal life as they had a small bit of land and no cattle. Lakhan had ploughed a piece of high land after borrowing a plough and a pair of bullocks. He had sowed hemp on this land. When the crop grew well, a herd of wild buffaloes came one night and ate it up. Lakhan was furious but he could not face a herd of wild buffaloes with his bamboo bow and only six arrows that he had. He, however, resolved to take revenge.

Lakhan went to the village blacksmith and in exchange for giving him help for a few days in his work got an iron bow from the blacksmith. He also made about twelve good arrows with sharp edges.

Lakhan's mother was not at all happy that Lakhan should go and shoot at the wild buffaloes. But Lakhan would not listen to her and taking her blessings, he left for the deeper portion of the jungle in the neighbourhood where he thought the buffaloes would surely be found. When night came Lakhan found a small hut in the midst of the jungle and found an old shrunken woman, the only inmate of the hut. From his instinct, Lakhan at once knew that she was a witch but as there was no other way out, Lakhan did *johar* (salutation) and told her, "Aunt, I will be staying with you tonight and you must share the little rice and some vegetables that I have brought." The old woman was very pleased at the bold and affectionate manner in which she was addressed and she could not possibly do any harm to Lakhan. She invited him inside the hut and they shared the food. Lakhan asked her as to where exactly the wild buffaloes lived. The witch asked as to why he was making this query and heard that the buffaloes had destroyed Lakhan's hemp crop. The witch gave Lakhan her blessings and told him that he had to go three miles west from her hut to reach the place where the wild buffaloes lived. But the old woman warned Lakhan that they were extremely fierce and it would be better if he watched them from the top of some tree nearby before he shot at them.

Next morning Lakhan left the hut and came to the place where the buffaloes rested at night. He waited there and somehow he felt like sweeping away the droppings and make the place clean. After cleaning the place towards the evening, he climbed up a tree. In the evening several herds of buffaloes came to the place and rested. There were hundreds of them and Lakhan shook in fear as to how he could shoot at the wild buffaloes and escape unhurt.

The night passed and in the morning the herds of wild buffaloes again went away. Lakhan got down and again cleaned the place by removing all the droppings and brought some water from a spring nearby and washed the place. He picked up some edible wild fruits and tubers and ate them. Again in the evening he took shelter on the tree and passed the night.

When the herds of wild buffaloes found that the place had been cleaned for the second day, they felt curious as to who was doing this. They left an old buffalo on the pretext that she was sick and could not move and asked the cow to find out the secret of what was happening. After the wild buffaloes left and finding that only one old buffalo was left alone, Lakhan made bold and came down. He cleaned and washed the whole place once again. He again collected some fruits for himself and quietly went up the tree before the evening came. When the buffaloes came back the old buffalo told them that a man was doing all this and he was perched on a tree in the neighbourhood. The buffaloes were grateful and told him to come down and swore not to kill him but to support him. Lakhan came down and it was arranged that he should stay at the sleeping place and keep it clean and whenever he wanted milk for his food he was to play on his bamboo flute and they would come at the sound.

This arrangement continued for some time. Every noon, Lakhan used to blow the flute and the buffaloes came and gave him much more milk than he wanted to drink. Lakhan even bathed himself in milk and this made his hair grow very long and shiny.

One day a parrot belonging to the local king saw him drying his long hair in the sun. The parrot went to the king and told him that it had found a husband for the king's daughter, a handsome young man with beautiful long hair. But no one could go near him as he lived with wild buffaloes. The king asked the parrot to find out some way and bring the young man to him so that he could give him his daughter in marriage. The parrot took the help of a crow. Both the parrot and the crow came to the hiding place of Lakhan and when the cows gave him milk at noon and he had put down his flute the crow seized it in his beak and went to the top of a tree. After the buffaloes left, Lakhan missed his flute and found the crow with it. He began to throw stones but the crow flew from tree to tree and seemed always just about to drop the flute and in this way enticed Lakhan on till he came to the king's palace. Lakhan followed the crow right inside and they shut the door on him and made him marry the princess.

Lakhan lived with the princess happily for a few days but his heart was with the wild buffaloes. A few days after, his wife's brothers began to talk rudely about him saying: "This fellow is a very poor man, without any relations and without any money. Why does he not think of going back to his people and to his own house with his wife. Everyone takes his bride to his own house." Lakhan heard this and wanted to teach them a lesson. He took up his flute and began to play on it. Within a few moments hundreds and hundreds of wild buffaloes rushed into the king's palace and at one signal of Lakhan gored to death every one they met excepting the aged king and his queen. The king was persuaded to give his kingdom to Lakhan.

Lakhan had not forgotten his old widow mother. When he became the king he went with his wife to the mother and brought her to his palace. They lived happily after that.

23

THE LAZY MAN

THE Santals as a class are hardy and active people. They would work hard the whole day in the fields or in the jungles and in the evening relax, play on the flutes or dance in the *akhar as* (the place where the villagers met for songs and dances and also to settle their disputes). A lazy man among the Santals is easily marked out and becomes the topic of gossip and ridicule. Even brothers would not spare if one of them was lazy and did not pull his weight in the domestic chores. But lazy men often become very clever and try to dodge men by their clever tricks. Kora, the youngest of three brothers in a small Santal village, was one such clever lazy man.

As Kora would not help the brothers he was often scolded. One day, however, the scolding annoyed him and Kora ran away from home. He had only a loin-cloth. It was winter and in the evening he began shivering with cold. He was happy to come to a village and find a group of herd-boys sitting round the fire in the village street and roasting wild rats. The Santals are very fond of eating roasted wild rats. Kora went up to them and sat down by the fire to warm himself. The herd-boys gave him some of the rats to eat and when they had finished their feast, the boys went off to their homes to sleep. Kora had no other place to go and as it was nice and warm by the fire, he made up his mind to sleep by the fire. At night a big dog came and coiled itself up on the warm ashes and also went to sleep alongside Kora. Although it was not at all pleasant, somehow, Kora managed to pass the night. Early morning the Headman of the village was passing that way to watch his fields. The Headman roused up Kora and asked who he was and if he did not find it very cold lying out in the open. Kora replied : "No, I never feel cold as my dog eats up all the cold. He could eat up the cold for hundreds of men." The Headman had a number of servants as he had a large quantity of fields. He at once thought that if he could get hold of the cold eating dog, he could do away with buying a number of thick sheets for the servants. He made an offer to buy the dog. Kora wanted five hundred rupees and ultimately the bargain was settled at one hundred rupees. The money was paid and the dog was made over to the Headman.

Kora immediately returned to his village with the money and gave it to his brothers. The brothers were surprised to see that their lazy brother could earn such a big sum in one night only.

Meanwhile, the Headman sent for his labourers and told them that he had found a valuable animal that would eat up the cold and would keep every one warm. That night the labourers were all put in one room and the dog was kept there too. The men in the hut shivered all night and in the morning the master found that he had been duped. In rage he got a stick and started beating the poor dog. The dog ran away. The Headman lost his money and was also laughed at by all the villagers for his folly.

But one hundred rupees would not keep Kora comfortable in the family for all time to come. He had lapsed into his laziness and would not work at all. There was again trouble in the family and Kora had to set out again on some other adventure.

When Kora left the hut and had gone a little way, he found a crab trying to burrow. Kora caught hold of the crab and took it along with him and tied it in his cloth. Kora walked the whole day and in the evening he came to a village. He camped for the night under a tree on the outskirts. The villagers came out and begged him to go and spend the night in one of the houses. Kora said: "Don't worry about me. I am not alone. I have a companion and we two shall be quite happy together." The villagers thought he was a peculiar man as they found no one else with him. However, they went back to their own huts.

Night came on and Kora untied the crab from his cloth and soon fell asleep. At about mid-night, a huge *Rakhas* (demon) came prowling along and seeing Kora sleeping alone made towards him. The faithful crab that was watching rushed at the *Rakhas* and quickly climbed up his body, seized his neck with its claws and slit the wind-pipe. Down fell the *Rakhas* and the noise awoke Kora. Kora took a big stone and dashed out the brain of the *Rakhas*. Kora cut off all the tips of the ears and tongue and claws and wrapped them up in his cloth and laid down to sleep again with the faithful crab in his bosom.

At dawn, the village watchman came on his round and found the *Rakhas* lying dead. This *Rakhas* was creating a lot of trouble and the king had declared a big reward if anybody could kill the *Rakhas*. The watchman went to the king and claimed the reward. The king himself came to the place where the *Rakhas* was lying. Kora had got up by then and when he heard the claim of the watchman he wanted the king to see as to why the *Rakhas* was without the tips of the ears, tongue and claws. The king was curious and Kora produced those parts and the crab. The crab quickly climbed up the body of the watchman and seized his neck with his claws and demonstrated how the wind-pipe of the *Rakhas* was slit. The watchman fell on his knees and admitted that his story was false. The king gave double the money he had promised as reward to Kora.

Kora went back home with the money and from then the brothers did not trouble him any more.

24

THE WIND AND THE SUN

THERE was a big dispute between the Wind and the Sun as to who was the more powerful. They saw a man going wrapped in a shawl and wearing a big *pagri* (head-gear). They asked the man to decide as to which one of them was the more powerful. The man told them: "Why do you quarrel? I will put you to a test. I am walking along with my shawl wrapped round me. I will see who can deprive me of the shawl and he will be the more powerful." The Wind wanted the first chance to try his luck. The Sun agreed. The Wind began to blow very hard and it was difficult for the man to walk but the result of the high wind was that the man wrapped his shawl more tightly round him to prevent it from being blown away and ultimately, fastened round the shawl with his *pagri*. The stronger the wind, the more attention he paid to the shawl and held it more tightly. The Wind gave up and asked the Sun to have his try. The Sun rose in the sky and beat upon the world with full force. The man began to perspire and took off his shawl and hung it on the stick he was carrying. The Wind had to admit defeat.

25

THE CLEVER MAN AND THE TIGER

DOWN the river Bansloi in Santal Parganas, there is a village Basatpur by the side of a thick forest. The king of Basatpur was a worried man as a man-eating tiger was harassing and killing the Santals whenever they would go into the forest to bring fuel or gather fruits, leaves and tubers. The Santals cannot possibly make a living unless they take help from the produce of the jungles. The king called together all his men and promised to give half of his kingdom to anyone who would kill the tiger. But no one accepted the offer.

A poor shikari lived in the neighbouring village. When he heard of the offer he decided to try his luck. He was a bachelor, without any dependants. He met the king and showed his willingness to go for the tiger but in return wanted not only half of his kingdom but also the princess. And as an evidence of his fulfilling the task, the shikari had to bring back either the dead tiger or bits of the tiger's ears and claws. The king agreed. Before leaving the palace the shikari was thoroughly searched.

The shikari collected his equipment and started off. In the jungle he went up a banyan tree as he was told that the tiger often come to relax under the tree.

At dawn the tiger came roaring under the tree and said: "Who's up there ? I smell a man !" The shikari replied: "It's me ! I smell the tiger for whom I waited through the night." The tiger was surprised, and said: "What for?" "I already have three or four like you in my circus party. I want you too so that I could earn money by taking you round the city. You wouldn't be harmed, I assure you. You will get meat everyday but will be tied to a chain." As the tiger did not see anyone of his kind around, he enquired about the others. The shikari climbed down the tree, uncovered a looking glass and made the tiger look through it. The clever shikari reflected the portraits of tigers he had brought with him, and said: "Are you satisfied now?" The tiger begged for mercy.

The shikari agreed to let the tiger free if the tiger left the jungle for good. The tiger agreed. The clever shikari wanted to cut the tiger's claws and tips of ears to ensure the tiger's exit from the jungle. The tiger agreed to this proposal too. The shikari cut the required parts and quickly climbed up the tree again. But the tiger proved true to his word and left the place. The shikari came back to the city and handed over parts of the tiger's body. The king gave him the promised reward.

Bansloi river still meanders through Santal Parganas. Basatpur village is also still there.

26

THE RAIBAR AND THE LEOPARD

ONCE a *raibar* (a mediator for marriage between a boy and a girl) was on his way to a distant village and had to pass through a thick forest. In the jungle he was confronted a leopard. The leopard asked the *raibar* to be ready to be killed. The *raibar* was frightened but did not lose his wits. He told the leopard : "Don't kill me, friend. I am going for an important work." The leopard asked about the work. The man answered : "I am making two men out of one."

The leopard was amazed and asked if he could make him into two and if so he would not touch him. The man replied : "This is very easy. Will you please get into the sack I am carrying and keep quiet until I ask you to speak." The leopard replied : "If you are successful, I will ask the entire race of leopards to spare the lives of *raibars*." So saying, the leopard got into the sack and the man tied it with a rope.

The man carried the sack on his head and threw it into the water of a river in the neighbourhood.

The man made his escape quickly thinking the leopard would be drowned. But the sack was picked up by a leopardess which sat watching the water of the river on the off chance of any big fish coming up for her food. The leopardess thought the sack was probably some animal which she could eat. When the leopardess found that there was a leopard in the sack she was greatly surprised. The leopard told her how he came into the sack and assured her that the *raibar's* prophecy was true as he had met her and she must be his mate. The leopardess was much impressed and the two lived together. The leopard proclaimed throughout the world of leopards that no *raibar* should be mauled when they go about arranging marriages.

But that is not the end of the story. Another day, the same *raibar* was passing through the jungle fully assured that the leopard he had met before was drowned. The same leopard met the man and greeted him as his great friend. The man was stupified and wanted to run away. The leopard, however, told him: "Well, you made two out of me. By throwing me into the water, you made me meet my mate and we now have two chubby cubs. I must give you some reward." The man collected his wits and wanted a fat deer to be killed and dragged near his house. The leopard agreed and got a fat deer for a feast, which the *raibar* held.

It is peculiar that *raibars* have never been injured by leopards although they have to go through thick forests in the land of the Santals while arranging marriages.

27

THE PRINCE AND THE SNAKE

A Santal prince was galloping to his wife's village to bring her to his house as she had come of age. The prince found a field of thatching grass on fire and in the middle there was a huge poisonous snake, unable to escape. The snake called out to him : "Prince, you are going to bring home your bride and I am going to be burnt alive. Please save me and if you do so I will give you a boon." The prince replied : "Snakes know not what gratitude is. If I save you I'll be killed". The snake replied : "I'm not that type. You save me and see what I do for you." The prince rode his horse and extinguished the fire. He then spread his *pagri* (headgear) over the embers so that the snake could crawl out. As soon as the snake came out, it said : "You are a fool and the world has no place for fools like you. You have saved a snake and now the snake is going to bite you." The prince pleaded that the matter should be referred to some judges. The snake agreed but did not want human beings to be referred to They set out together and came near a big banyan tree. The banyan tree was asked if the snake was right in killing the prince, whose life the prince had saved. The banyan tree replied, "I don't see why the snake should not eat you up. Men enjoy the shade of the trees and then lop off their branches. It is only right that the snake should kill you."

There was a cow grazing and the cow was

made the next judge. But the cow replied : "I don't see why the snake should not kill you. See how men treat us. They take our milk, beat us and make us work hard and when we are dry our calves are taken away."

The prince was bewildered. There was a tank nearby. He thought that the tank would come to his help. They put the same question to the tank. The tank replied : "Mankind returns evil for good. I give them water to drink and to irrigate the fields. Instead of being grateful, men spit into me and wash dirty things in me. Why should the snake not return you evil for good ?"

Having lost his case before the three judges the prince was asked to be ready for death. The prince pleaded that he should be allowed to meet his wife before he is killed. The snake granted him liberty to do so. The prince went to his wife's place but could not join the mirth and feast that followed because of obvious reason. He narrated the story to his wife who asked him not to worry, and that she would accompany him on his return journey. The prince agreed. On the way the prince and his bride saw the snake. The bride asked the snake to kill her before her husband was killed as she had no place to live after her husband's death. The snake asked her to return to her parents but she refused to do so. The snake promised her a *mantra* (incantation) by means of which she could support herself. The snake whispered a *mantra* and told her that if she took some dust in her hand and repeated the *mantra* and then blew on the dust, any person on whom she sprinkled the dust would at once be burnt to ashes. She was also given a *mantra* for restoring people to life. The clever girl wanted to try the first *mantra* on the snake itself and told the snake that she wanted to test it. The experiment was made on a tree and was successful.

Soon after when the snake was rushing towards the prince with its crest raised, the bride gathered some dust, repeated the *mantra*, blew and threw it on the snake who was immediately reduced to ashes. The prince and his wife went away and lived happily thereafter.

28

THE QUEEN WHO WAS POSSESSED

THIS is about two Santals—Mangru and Sukra. Mangru got the name because he was born on a Tuesday (Mangal) and as Sukra was born on a Friday (Shukra), he also got the name the same way. The two once came across a witch-doctor who had given them some *mantras* (incantations) to please the God. By reciting these *mantras* hundreds of times they came to possess a power by which they could order the tigers and snakes to come to them at any time from the forest. They would utilise the tigers to till their fields. The tigers were yoked to the plough and the snakes were used as ropes.

The son of the local king was possessed by a strange illness and no medicine could cure him. The king asked Mangru and Sukra to cure the prince. They both touched the prince and pronounced that the king's second queen had bewitched the child. On their advice the king locked her up in a rocky cave where she would scream day and night. The king wanted to get rid of her. Mangru and Sukra set the cave on fire in order to destroy her. When the flames approached her she screamed that she was leaving the child. Within moments the prince was cured. But during this process the queen also got freed from the evil *Bonga* who was possessing her. She was now a changed person. The king amply rewarded both of them.

The Santals have a great belief in witches and their evil influence on men but they also believe that the witches can be controlled and driven away. This story, in a different shape; is also current among the Mundas of Chhota Nagpur.

29

THE GHORMUHAS

EVERY Santal child is afraid of the ghormuhas because right from the childhood he is constantly told that if he tries to be naughty he will be thrown to the ghormuhas who would eat him up.

The ghormuhas have heads like horses. A *ghora* is a horse. With heads like horses, ghormuhas have bodies and arms like men but they have only one leg. They love human beings as their food.

One day Somai, a young Santal, was hunting a deer and the deer ran away to that particular part of the forest where the ghormuhas lived. In his craze to get the deer, Somai got into that part and was immediately caught and taken to the dens of the ghormuhas for being eaten up. First, the ghormuhas smoked him for two or three days to make his meat tender and to drive away all the vermins from his body. They fed him well everyday with rice cooked with turmeric and gave him delicious pieces of boiled wild tubers and *sag* (spinach) so that he got fat and tender. Somai was watching how they dealt with their other victims. The victims were tied hand and foot and thrown alive into the pot of boiling oil so that they are well cooked. The body was not, however, split into pieces but cooked whole. The bodies were hung up in the doorway and the ghormuhas would take a bite as they passed in and out.

Somai also found that the ghormuhas were so heartless that they would eat their own parents too! He picked up a saying from the ghormuhas, "The pumpkin growing on our roof has got ripe and is due to fall and burst. Let us burst it and eat it." The pumpkin was one of the old parents and the saying meant that the parent is now too old and as such should be killed and feasted upon.

Somai saw all this and was terribly frightened. The ghormuhas could run very fast and they used to make the victims run a race with them everyday. Their plan was that they would eat him when he was quick and strong enough to beat them in the race. In course of time Somai was able to beat them in running on the road. The ghormuhas decided that they would now make him run in the fields and if he could beat them there they would eat him up.

Somai came to know of their plan. He decided to run away. If he stayed there, he would be eaten up and if they caught him up running away, he was to meet the similar fate. But there was a chance of life in the latter. The first day they raced in the fields. Somai was winning but he remembered their plan and stopped himself and let himself be beaten that day. He resolved to try and escape the next day. The ghormuhas were also restive and wanted to make a feast of him and secretly decided that they woul deat him up the next day whatever happened. So the next day, when the race began Somai dashed off towards the lower lands where the rice fields had embankments. Withh is two legs Somai jumped the embankments easily and ran fast. The ghormuhas with their one leg could not jump well and tumbled and fell. When the ghormuhas could cross the embankments, Somai was beyond the land of ghormuhas. Now the ghormuhas had their limits of power and they could not go beyond certain zones. Somai after his escape told men what ghormuhas were like and how they lived. From that day the story of the ghormuhas has spread and the Santals are careful to avoid the area where the ghormuhas live.

30

RAMAI AND SOMAI

FISHING in the streamlets in Santal Parganas, particularly when there is a rush of water is a great pastime with the Santal youths. They do fishing with small baskets made of cane For fishing many would leave their other works like ploughing or grazing cattle although the return in money for the whole day's catch is small.

There were two poor men, Ramai and Somai in a village near Maheshpur in Santal Parganas. They used to sell their labour in the weekly *hat* at Maheshpur. On other days, they would accept any other odd job.

They made bold and took some waste land from the Headman. In Santal Parganas, there are still lots and lots of wasteland. According to the custom of the area, the bit of wasteland that is ploughed first by a man will go to him. Both Ramai and Somai were very happy when the Headman of the village (*Pradhan* as he is called) gave them permission to plough two plots of wasteland. They ploughed up the land but as they could only borrow cows and not bullocks and the plough-shares were very small, they could only sow millet. In Santal Parganas borrowing of bullocks for tilling the land is quite common. In that case the borrower has to work in the field of the lender of the bullocks for one or two days. If bullocks are not available, cows are yoked to the plough for cultivation.

After some time the rains came and the streamlets were full of water in which tiny fish played. The temptation to catch fish was too great for Somai to stick to cultivation. He neglected the millet he had sown and started fishing. For some time he could make good profit by selling the fish he had caught. But the streamlets would get full of water only when the rains came. So there were breaks but Somai would not come to the field at all. Ramai stuck to the field and paid every attention to the millet he had sown. He also cleared some more wasteland and sowed maize and rice. Somai would taunt Ramai and used to tell him that he had better take to fishing which gave quick and easy return.

After the rains were over, there was no more fishing to be done. Somai found that the bit of wasteland he had taken was full of weeds and bushes and the crops he had grown were all eaten up by cattle. Somai was left to starve and had to go from village to village offering to work as a labourer. But Ramai cut his millet and lived on that till his maize was ripe. The maize supported him until his rice was ready and so he always had plenty to eat. Somai had the lesson of his life and came and wept at Ramai's place one day. Ramai gave him a part of his seeds of different crops and helped him to plough his bit of wasteland once again.

Maheshpur is a prosperous large village in Santal Parganas now and famous for the cattle market held there every week.

31

THE THIEF'S SON

PILFERING of goats when there is no one near about is not uncommon in Santal Parganas. Once upon a time a goat had strayed into the house of a villager who promptly killed it and hid the body. After some time the owner of the goat came in search of it. The man who had killed the goat denied and even invited the owner of the missing animal to look into the goat-house in case the goat had got mixed up with his goats.

In the night the thief brought out the body and cooked it. All his family members had a good meal. The thief told his sons that next morning when they would be grazing the cattle they should not go near any, one so that others should not smell that they had eaten meat. Next morning the thief's son took his goats out for grazing but carefully avoided his friends, keeping them at a distance. The friends thought it was rather funny. The thief's son said that he had been warned by his father that they should not be allowed to smell what he had eaten. His friends asked: "What have you eaten?" The simpleton said that he had eaten goat's flesh. This story got out and the owner of the lost goat came to the thief's house again and found that there were remnants of the goat. The matter was taken to the Panchayat and the thief was fined one rupee four annas and was asked to give another goat in exchange.

32

TAKING A FORBIDDEN NAME

AMONG the Santals the husband and the wife do not normally mention each other's name. A man should not call his younger brother's wife or his wife's elder sister by name. Women should not use the name of their younger sister's husband or that of their husband's elder brother. Although the custom is slowly disappearing, it is still there. There are some folk tales connected with this custom and how men make fools of themselves by sticking to this custom.

There was a man, Rama, who went to plough his field. After he had done so, he found he had not brought the seed with him. He called for his wife pretending, however, that he was speaking to his daughter: "Daughter, seed, seed!" The wife shouted back: "Are you going to sow it?" (*Eram*—will you sow?). Every time Rama called out for seed, she answered, "Eram". He lost his temper and went to his house and asked his wife as to why he had taken his name when he wanted the seed for sowing. The husband was almost going to give a good thrashing to the wife. His wife said to him: "What a fine fellow you are! Why did you have a name which is the same as the word for 'sow'? I only wanted to know if the seed was for sowing. I'd no idea to take your name. Funny!" Rama had a good laugh and told his wife: "How could I help it, as my father and mother had given me the name?" The matter ended there. Rama's elder brother heard about the quarrel and told them that there was another custom: if anyone is compelled to use the forbidden word, he or she should spit on the ground first and then take the name.

Once a man called Dhuju went to the field and his brothers had to follow him. It had been arranged that they should sow *gundli* (a small grained millet) in the field. Dhuju came to the field with the bullocks ready and waited for his brothers for some time. As the brothers did not turn up, he began to call, "Pal, ho." (Pal: plough-share)

It so happened that the wife of the younges brother had the same name, Palo. Just at that moment when the eldest brother was shouting for the *pal* (plough-share), Palo the youngest brother's wife had gone towards the field to throw away the dirt from the cow shed. Palo thought that Dhuju was calling her by the name, which was forbidden. She felt embarrassed, came back home and kept sullen. When the brothers came home for food, Palo would not talk to her husband. The husband thought there was some quarrel between the women of the house and he did not take much notice. The mother-in-law soon found that Palo had refused to take food and was going about with a long face. The mother-in-law asked Palo as to what the matter was. After some coaxing, Palo told her as to what had happened. She complained that her husband's elder brother had shouted her name and had insulted her. She said that the neighbours might have heard it and would think that she was a shameless girl.

When the mother asked Dhuju as to why he had called Palo, his younger brother's wife by name, Dhuju was at first taken aback and then saw through the joke. He explained as to what had happened and said that he was shouting: "Pal, ho", and not Palo. The misunderstanding was cleared. Palo, the youngest brother's wife, came and touched Dhuju's feet as she had done on the day of her marriage and Dhuju gave her his blessings.

If the mistake had not been explained and if some neighbours had complained that Dhuju called Palo, his younger brother's wife, there was every chance of Palo's being turned out of the family and the village as a bad woman.

33

THE GOOD LESSON

TWO Santal boys were great friends. As they grew, one of them married a richer Santal's daughter and became a *ghar-damad* (a son-in-law who stays permanently in the father-in-law's house and is treated like a son). The other friend remained poor and lived by scraping a little land and owning one or two goats. In course of time the *ghar-damad* boy inherited all his father-in-law's land, house and cattle.

The poor friend visited his rich friend after many years. The rich friend showed his poor friend all his lands and a big tank which he had dug out and said it was full of fish. But in the evening the food that was given was just a little rice with some *sag*. The poor friend ate heartily. While they were smoking after the dinner, the poor friend made a good joke. He told his friend: "My friend, you had a good one pulled on me. Whose lands and tank you showed as yours? I almost thought they really belonged to you." The rich friend got rather surprised and said: "Why, they actually belong to me. Why should you doubt it?" The poor friend replied: "If all that were yours, surely I would have got better type of rice and good fish." Saying so, the poor friend laughed. His rich friend was greatly embarrassed.

34

ENIGMAS

THE Santals, like many of the other aboriginals, are very fond of riddles. Very often when the Santal boys retire in the night and smoke together under the sky or under a big tree, they will be putting riddles to one another by turn. Some folk tales are also based on such riddles. The following is a very common folk tale based on enigmas.

Once upon a time a man and his son went to the house of the son's in-laws in another village. The visit was unexpected but the father-in-law took it in a nice manner although he felt that he did not have anything particular to entertain his guests. He called one of his daughters and said: "Now, my dear girl, I'm going for a bath and will come back with a potful of the water of dry land for these friends. You fill the little river and the big river while I'm away; polish the big axe and the little axe and dig out five or six channels. Bar the friends into the cow-house." So saying he went away for his bath. The two visitors were wondering as to what it all meant. They did not like the talk about axes and digging channels and barring them in the cow-house. The boy told his father that his father-in-law meant evil and had probably been possessed by some evil *Bonga* (spirit) and he wanted to kill them. The father advised that both of them should get up and run away. They started moving when the young girl ran after them and called them back. They asked her as to what her father meant to do. She laughed at their folly and explained that what her father meant was that she should wash their feet and give them a seat in the cow-house, and make ready two pots of rice beer and polish the big and little brass basins, make five or six leaf-cups as he would bring back some liqour and they would all have a drink. At this explanation, they had all a hearty laugh and came back to the house.

35

THE FASTIDIOUS WIFE

A young Santal bride used to feel ashamed of her husband as he had a large tumour on his forehead. She refused to go out with him to dances and other social functions for fear of being laughed at. The husband nursed a grievance about this and wanted to teach a lesson to his wife in an indirect way.

The *Charaka-Puja* came. During Charaka-Puja, *melas* (fairs) are held in different villages but Rajmahal town's fair was always the main attraction. The town was about 10 *kos* (1 *kos* means two miles) from the village. The young wife made a party of her own with some other women and went to see the mela and to join the dances. Her husband was keen to go but she said in that case she would not go.

After the wife had left, the husband also slipped out, dressed for the mela with a big *pugri* (head gear) on but without covering the big tumour. He reached the mela and joined some men and women in a dance, which goes about in circles. He saw from a little distance that his wife was also dancing in another circle.

The clever husband managed that the circle in which he was dancing should go near the circle of men and women where his wife was. The two circles came very close to each other and the wife was surprised to see that her husband had been accepted so well and no one was laughing at him because of his tumour. After the dance was over, the embarrassed wife approached her husband and said that she would be in his company for the other dances.

The small cloud between the husband and the wife vanished in no time.

36

THE PAHARIA SOCIALISTS

BEFORE the Santals came to Santal Parganas, the whole country was a dense jungle and the *Paharias*, an earlier aboriginal race, peopled the Santal Parganas areas. There was a big Paharia king with the four *taluqs* (big areas) of Sankara, Chiptiam, Sulunga and Dhaka. The Paharia king was named Somar Singh and he used to pay tribute to the king of Burdwan.

Once Somar Singh sent the annual tribute through ten Paharias with a headman. They went to Burdwan, paid the tribute and the king of Burdwan gave them a feast comprising meat and liqour. They were provided a comfortable room to sleep in but with just one cot.

When the group of ten Paharias retired, they had a good talk among themselves as to who was going to sleep on the cot. At last they decided that no one should sleep on the cot and they would all sleep on the floor and put their feet on the bed. The idea was that they could feel that they all had an equal share of the bed.

In the morning the Burdwan king came in and found them all lying in the strange position with their feet on the cot. The king was very much amused. He told them that the bed was meant for the Headman and asked if they had no distinctions of rank.

The Headman proudly replied : "Yes, we observe distinctions in our own villages. Here we are in a foreign land and we are all equal. We don't observe any distinction now."

The king was bewildered and made his apologies.

37

THE KING OF THE BHUYANS

THE Bhuyans are a race separate from the Santals. There was once a king of the Bhuyans who had his palace near a Santal village. The king was very friendly with the Santals and was a great friend of the Santal *Parganait* and the *Manjhi*. The Parganait is the tribe-head of a group of Santal villages. The Manjhi is the head of a Santal village and his duty is to collect the rents and also to work as the village police officer. The Manjhi has to report crimes. His assistant is known as *Parmanik*.

The Bhuyan king always listened to the advice of the Manjhi and the Parganait. The Santals and Bhuyans lived happily under this particular king.

Unfortunately on the king's death, his son became the king and was a very severe master. He soon fell out with the Santals. He did not listen to the Parganait or to the Manjhi and if any cattle or buffaloes were found grazing anywhere near his crops, he would put them in the pound or beat the cowherds severely. The Santals got very angry and longed to get even with the king. They were looking for an excuse to pay back the king in the same coin.

Usually, after the paddy is cut and before the millet crop is gathered, the youths and maidens of the Santal village have a dance. Once they danced all night. They thought that it was not worthwhile going to sleep and they had better take the cattle out to graze at once. They did so.

In the noon the cowherds were very sleepy after dancing the whole night and they all fell fast asleep on the bare ground. The buffaloes moved out and grazed on a field of millet belonging to the king. The king ordered the *Sipahis* (policemen) to go and beat the cowherds. The cowherds ran away but the village *Parmanik* did not run away and instead went to drive the cattle out of the field. He thought he must do his duty even at the cost of his life.

The *Sipahis* fell upon him but when they were going to beat him a big cobra came rustling up behind them. The *Sipahis* ran for their life and the *Parmanik* drove the cattle home.

The king was very angry at the escape of the cowherds, particularly the *Parmanik*. He told his *Sipahis* to give the cowherds a thrashing when the cattle were brought home the next day. The *Sipahis* did so. But while they gave a good beating to the other cowherds they did not dare lay their hands on the *Parmanik* as they thought they might be bitten by the snake. The *Parmanik* went back home and told the villagers what had happened to other boys.

The Santals went together and complained to the king and took up a threatening attitude. The king told them that he would make all the cowherd boys jump up and run to their villages. The Santals carried the wounded boys who were almost senseless. The king got some good hot chillies and asked the *Sipahis* to thrust the chilly paste up their noses. This was done and the smarting soon made the cowherd boys jump up and run away in a lively fashion. The king kept his word and cured them.

The Santals, however, left their villages and went to another jungle where they reclaimed fallow lands and settled themselves. The king lost a good bit of revenue and came to his senses.